MW01268345

The Legal Matrix
How the System is Controlling Your Life!

By Attorney William Dawson

Copyright

ISBN 0-9769915-1-9

I thank the Lord Jesus Christ for using me as a vessel to do His work. I truly believe that my practice and reach is my ministry. All my work and effort is dedicated to the loving memory of my mother, Annie L. Dawson. Additionally, I especially thank the loves of my life Wayne, Elsie, Crystal, Tammy, and Danielle, Lavern, Karina, McKenna, Trace and all my other family for your love and support.

I also thank all the Neo's listed in this book, one way, or another; you have touched my life and given me inspiration to strive for greatness. Specifically I thank those who have inspired and pushed this work - Airica, Melissa, Sherry, Sonya for listening and enduring. Nicole "CoCo", Maurise, Tremia, Dushawn for staying on me. Donshawn, Ken, BJ, Will, Roscoe, Garrett, Fernando, Orlando, Nate Bishko my road dogs. Ilinda Reese, Herb Thomas, G. Lewis, Dr. Malcom Walters, Gary and Jillian Warner, Ron Harper, Bishop Moultry, Darlene White and Michelle Early.

The Neo List: Judge Keenon, Judge Cox, Judge Groves, Judge Mays, Judge Tarver, Judge Moore, Judge Greene, Judge Saffold, Judge Russo and Gladys, Judge Gaul, Judge Nicastro, Bill Mason and Jerry Dowling – the Youth Intervention Program is a great effort, Byron Wasko, Rufus Sims, Scott Ramsey, Ed Wade, Ryan Benjamin, Mark Marein, John Carson, James Willis, Myron Watson, Pastor Rowan, Pastor Vernon and the Word Church – true visionaries, The East Cleveland Public Schools, The East Cleveland Municipal Court 2005, Eric Brewer the Power Broker.

If anyone has been left out, blame my mind, not my heart. There are Neo's and people I care about who were not listed in this book, you know who you are because everyday you work to change the lives of your communities, families and the world. This book could not possibly list every one of you; nevertheless, your hard work is noted and appreciated.

About Attorney Dawson

Attorney William Dawson practices law in the State of Ohio county and federal courts. His practice includes criminal law, personal injury, business, entertainment, domestic relations, and bankruptcy. In addition to the practice of law, writing and speaking, Attorney Dawson is also the director of the Annie L. Dawson Foundation for Justice, Education, and Achievement which focuses on enriching the lives of our youth and bringing an end to the cycle of negativity and destruction.

Other Services Provided

Through seminars and presentations, Attorney Dawson has developed *The Legal Matrix* and *The Legal Matrix Workbook* with accompanying material to address:

- Dealing with Emotionalism
- Understanding of the Legal System
- Staying out of Jail

William Dawson, Attorney at Law, 3401 Enterprise Parkway, Suite 340, Beachwood Ohio, 44122 tele: (216) 766-5777 fax: (216) 691-9520
www.matrixtheory.com, www.legalmatrix.org

The Table of Contents

Introduction

As I sit in Federal Court, waiting for a judge to sentence my client on a drug possession case, I fully understand and appreciate the dynamics of the Legal Matrix. The Courts and Judges (for the most part) are faceless Agents, doing the work of the Legal Matrix, keeping the system up and going, controlling our everyday lives and activities. When it comes to the Legal Matrix and how it can affect our lives, and more specifically the way it is about to affect my client, it seems that too many people fail to understand that selling or possessing cocaine, or crack can lead to mandatory terms of imprisonment. Until faced with the possibility of long term prison, the hustler on the street, attempting to take care of his/her family, does not respect the risk of incarceration and the heartless way in which justice is administered.

In *The Matrix* movie, Morpheous says that "you are a slave, born into a prison you can not taste or touch – a prison for your mind." The Legal Matrix stretches far beyond criminal law; it touches every area of our lives encompassing all laws and regulations. Take for instance two people who enter in to a relationship, with all the passion and excitement that new love can bring, they cannot foresee that the same relationship that brings joy can lead to pain through divorce, separation, domestic violence, child support disputes and a myriad of other problems and heartache.

From these situations, and many more, you can find yourself in the grasp of The Legal Matrix. From driving a car to the decisions we make in regard to our children, the Legal Matrix is a system that will catch you and control your life. Simple knowledge of this fact leads to empowerment.

Even though the intent of the Legal Matrix is to control our lives, the system is not perfect. In fact the Legal Matrix, in its goal to control, often makes mistakes. In May of 2004 the FBI apologized for falsely linking an Oregon lawyer to a Madrid, Spain terrorist bombing. The FBI fingerprint experts proclaimed that lawyer Brandon Mayfield was a suspect in the Madrid train bombings six days after the attacks. Attorney Mayfield, a Muslim convert, was arrested and detained for two weeks before Spanish police confirmed that the fingerprint belonged to another man. His lawyer believes the government used his Muslim connections to prejudice the grand jury and to obtain a warrant against him[i].

On the legal front in America, Richard Clarke who was the former counterterrorism head under the Bush and Clinton administration, started a political and emotional controversy with the publishing of his book *Against All Enemies* and his appearance before the current 9/11 Investigating Committee. He caused major controversy when, through his book *Against All Enemies,* he exposed the Legal Matrix, and the behind the scene workings of the Legal Matrix to cover up mistakes, to shape facts, support specific positions and fight to censor anyone who speaks out against it.

It is against that back drop I begin on this journey of justice for all. This is not an anti law or anti government piece. Instead it is a search for truth and the extreme desire to help the unaware. I have been practicing for a long time, fighting the fight for justice continuously, at least in my mind. Even when I worked for a corporate firm, it was obvious that my interest was to ensure that justice was received by everyone. Initially it started out as a mission for African Americans, but very soon became a mission for all mankind. I realize the injustices African Americans have faced, and continue to face, are no different from any other person who becomes a victim of the system. The bottom line is that if we allow other people to get pounded by the system, it will happen to all of us. I fight and I take it personally. Otherwise, attorneys would allow opportunities to slip by, allow evidence to go unnoticed, and allow innocent people to get convicted.

The Legal Matrix's design is really simple: laws, rules and regulations are in place. They dictate our total existence. It is not designed to give us absolute freedom. We can work with in the design to achieve success, peace, and freedom. Don't underestimate the Legal Matrix – the design will take away your life and liberty in a heart beat

The Legal Matrix will follow the format of *The Matrix* movie. Those who saw *The Matrix* are aware that it was more than a science fiction film; it was a journey through some of life's mysteries. Mysteries of science, religion, and beliefs. The Matrix's attempt to look into the depths of knowledge and understanding is parallel to the way in which we must approach our lives. As in the movie there is a greater system around us that most of us are unaware of. Most are not aware that, to some extent, we are controlled. In order to understand the system and work within it to achieve our goals and life's purpose, we must know the system. The system is the Legal Matrix.

> *"Life is a great and noble game between the citizen and the government. The government nearly always scores, but the citizen should not thereby be discouraged. Even if he always loses the game, it is in his power to inflict a considerable amount of annoyance on the victors."* - Rose McCaulay

I am here, not because of the path that lies before me, but because of the path that lies behind me. - Morpheous, in The Matrix Reloaded

The Legal Matrix

> The old saying that "knowledge is power" is not just a cliché but the only way to survive in the Legal Matrix. If more people had knowledge of The Legal Matrix and the laws and events that will bring you subject to The Legal Matrix, this would be a more lawful society.

The Flow Through the Legal Matrix

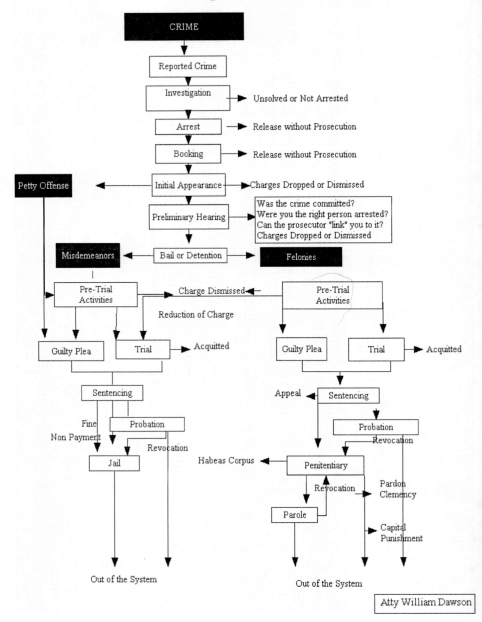

CRIME

Reported Crime

Investigation → Unsolved or Not Arrested

Arrest → Release without Prosecution

Booking → Release without Prosecution

Petty Offense ← Initial Appearance → Charges Dropped or Dismissed

Preliminary Hearing → Was the crime committed?
Were you the right person arrested?
Can the prosecutor "link" you to it?
Charges Dropped or Dismissed

Misdemeanors ← Bail or Detention → Felonies

Pre-Trial Activities → Charge Dismissed ← Pre-Trial Activities

Reduction of Charge

Guilty Plea | Trial → Acquitted | Guilty Plea | Trial → Acquitted

Sentencing | Appeal ← Sentencing

Fine | Probation | Probation
Non Payment | Revocation | Revocation

Jail | Habeas Corpus ← Penitentiary | Pardon Clemency

Revocation

Parole | Capital Punishment

Out of the System | Out of the System

Atty William Dawson

6

Chapter I

What is the Legal Matrix?

Technically speaking, Matrix is an acronym for the The Multi-state Anti-Terrorism Information Exchange (MATRIX) which allows police to fight crime by processing information through a database that combines various sources of information and the criminal records of individuals. The Matrix is really a replacement of the Pentagon's attempt to establish a national network with the purpose to fight terrorism through investigative techniques. This national system appears to be a little different than the Pentagon's system because it is being implemented on a state by state basis and is supposedly voluntary.

Beyond the governmental definition, in reality the Legal Matrix is all around us. It exists when we sleep, when we're shopping, while caring for our children, even when we're doing nothing at all. While we are fixated on everyday activities, the things that spark our individual interest, we are oblivious to the war that is being fought beneath us, on top of us and all around us. It is a war against disorder, crime, and terrorism versus the fight for civil liberties, freedom and personal success.

The Legal Matrix is a system designed to keep us under control. By *control* I am referring to the control system necessary for organized living. I am not referring to another conspiracy theory, instead I am revealing the truth about the world in which we exist and how we are effected by the legal system whether we acknowledge it or not. Many of us are aware that laws exist. Those with the basic knowledge often spend a lot of time criticizing and complaining about the legal system and its laws. However, as an American entrepreneur Damon Dash put it, "You can't criticize what you don't understand." So it is important for us to understand this system that is often and justifiably criticized.

On a practical level, the Legal Matrix consists of the rules that we live by, the rules that cause us to be accused of crimes. It is after we are accused of disobeying the rules of the Legal Matrix, that the Legal Matrix takes full effect. After breaking a law, we are possibly arrested, interrogated, formally charged, forced to hire a lawyer, spend money on defense, face the possibility of conviction, sentencing, jail time, post conviction release and a life time stigma. That is the Legal Matrix.

Individually and even collectively, we all want the same thing – freedom of thought, freedom of expression and success. It does not matter how we define success, we all want to achieve some set of goals. What many people have failed to realize is that in order to achieve and experience true success, we must operate within The Legal Matrix. No one person is exempt from its consequences. If you don't believe me just ask Kobe Bryant, Jason Williams, Michael Jackson, Rush Limbaugh or countless famous people fighting in the legal system. Our success in the Legal Matrix depends on our ability to understand that our entire society is law. Law encompasses every part of our lives.

To be successful, we need to know the beginning of the law, the inner workings of the law, the effects of the Legal Matrix and, most importantly, how to coexist in this Legal Matrix without becoming its victim.

Once we travel down the path to understanding the system, we will find that some rules can be bent, others broken. Nevertheless, success in the Legal Matrix is about knowing the path versus walking the path. Together we will uncover the truth. As was told to Neo in *The Matrix* movie, now you have a choice. You can take the blue pill and go back to your regular life or take the red pill and see how deep the rabbit hole goes. It's all about choices!

As far as laws are concerned, the Legal Matrix encompasses the following:

1. Laws in General – Shortly after the Abu Ghraib prison abuse scandal broke, several shocking United States government internal memorandums surfaced. The memos, in effect, offered complex legal arguments to justify the U.S.'s failure to abide by the major international and national laws prohibiting torture.

An August 2002 Department of Justice (DOJ) memorandum revealed a very narrow definition of "torture" the President could legally adopt. Under this definition, the only treatment that would count as torture would have to be "equivalent in intensity to the pain accompanying serious physical injury, such as organ failure, impairment of bodily function, or even death." Ballotpaper.org, August 2004.

In addition, a March 6, 2003 draft report prepared by Pentagon lawyers also defined torture narrowly – and also offered arguments as to why United States government Agents who torture prisoners could not be prosecuted. The draft report made the nearly-ridiculous suggestion that if the purpose of the torture was to extract information, not to cause pain, it wasn't really torture: "Even if the defendant [United States government agent] knows that severe pain will result from his actions," it suggests, "if causing such harm is not his objective, he lacks the requisite specific intent even though the defendant did not act in good faith." Ballotpaper.org, August 2004. These events suggest that laws are created and manipulated daily to keep the Legal Matrix going.

2. The Drug Laws – The drug laws cover permissible and illegal drugs, the excuses allowing use of certain drugs and the penalties for using, possessing, or selling others.

3. Relationships, Domestic Relations and the side effects – The when, where and how to enter into a legal relationship. The governing of relationships, the division of money, property, time and parental rights.

4. Traffic Laws – The questions of who can drive, when and where they can drive, and ultimately the revocation of the ability to drive.

5. Politics – Who can vote, where to vote and when (or if) those votes will be counted.

6. Government – The actual running of this system of laws and control of the people in America.

7. Everything else – Every situation and circumstance in our life is governed by laws.

This list does not exhaust all the laws that exist. The aim is to help bring about an understanding that every area of our lives has a form of governance and rules we must follow. These rules are what make up the Legal Matrix.

To understanding the existence of The Legal Matrix, there are elements that must be discussed to help shape your understanding. There are choices, laws, rules, people who enforce the laws, people who work for the betterment and freedom of all people and systems that must be played.

The Red Pill

In *The Matrix* movie, Neo, while sitting with Morpheous, was given the choice of taking one of two pills. The blue pill, which would return him back to his regular life, and the red pill which would give him ultimate knowledge. This scene in the movie is similar to the choice we have in our lives. We have the option of living life without knowledge of the system, thereby, being moved by life's events like a ship without a rudder. The red pill, on the other hand, gives knowledge, not just regular book knowledge, but the knowledge that is hidden away in the back rooms and secret societies in America. Knowledge that is seemingly available to certain people in the right place at the right time or with the right connections.

Concerning the choice between the blue pill, (blissful ignorance), and the red pill (true knowledge) many philosophy classes have conducted research to determine whether more people would choose ignorance or knowledge, deception or the harsh reality of life. Research reveals that the majority of people chose the blue pill preferring a life of blissful ignorance. The blue pill keeps us unaware of the harsh reality and allows us to live our lives peacefully, without worry, without involvement or commitment to a greater cause – freedom. There is nothing wrong with that choice; we know that it takes a lot of sacrifice to pass comfort for struggle. Most of us are comfortable living a life of conformity. We have been traveling through life moving with the tide, instead of controlling our direction or guiding our own paths. We go through life not asking any questions, just taking things as they are presented to us. If we reach a bump in the road or get into any kind of trouble, we deal with the consequences by hiring an attorney and getting pushed around the system. Often this life choice, the blue pill, leaves us on the side lines of life complaining about and being a victim of the system instead of changing the tide.

The other alternative, the red pill (true knowledge) is a choice that few desire. Choosing to know the truth of the system in which we live and dealing with its reality takes a lot of guts and may lead to serious sacrifice. Some would say that it's difficult to know the truth and not get involved to promote a better way of life. Taking the red pill is making a choice to get involved.

Taking the red pill is reading this book, attending the Legal Matrix seminars and conducting independent studies. Taking the red pill is also determining the part you play in the Legal Matrix; coexisting with it and learning what you can do to change the Legal Matrix – win the war. Just as in *The Matrix* movie, the red pill leading to knowledge of the Legal Matrix is hard to swallow. A metamorphosis will take place. Things will be seen differently because you will no longer be looking at life with sunglasses on, being shielded from reality. As Morpheous told Neo, "you have never used them (your eyes) before." Your mind will be sore, and your head and heart will hurt. The truth is hard to except.

Reality is not too pretty, but at the same time it is not all bad. We can be happy while having knowledge of the Legal Matrix. We can be happy while living with the Legal Matrix. With knowledge of the Legal Matrix comes the goal for each of us to win the war. To win the war we must make sure the Legal Matrix works for us and not against us. Making sure that it helps secure our rights and does not diminish them, to ensure that we are truly protected and not quietly violated. It is only in the environment of secured rights and protections that we can pursue and achieve all of our goals.

Welcome to knowledge. The red pill is knowledge. Welcome to the journey of uncovering the secrets of the Legal Matrix, and learning how to be successful within the system.

There are no tricks to the system, its just about learning the ins and outs so that we can be successful.

Chaos

In the very beginning, before there were kings and queens, man existed in what can be considered a lawless society. Biblically speaking God punished his chosen people for the lawless activities and chaos in which they were living in the early days. A modern day example would be the situation in Iraq after the 2003 United States entry to remove Sadaam Hussein from power. In Iraq, the daily news reported accounts of Americans being killed, the lack of government, law, lawyers, and libraries. Even though the United States is attempting to help re-establish a lawful society in Iraq, it is a difficult process that will ultimately take a long time to accomplish and cost millions of dollars and lives. There is no one who would disagree with the assertion, that conditions in modern day Iraq make normal peaceful life impossible. There is little opportunity to achieve meaningful success, prosperity or peace.

The same situation existed for all of mankind in the beginning. Of course there are historians who will disagree and claim that the early times were filled with people cooperating, getting along and using resources harmoniously. However, it can not be denied that in early times there was less structure and more chaos.

In comparison, let's fast forward to America's early years. The time when the government began molding the Legal Matrix that exists to this day. Step by step, mistake by mistake and accomplishment by accomplishment it has truly been a building block process. From the control of African Americans and other immigrants to the strengthening of the police force, in the government's view, chaos was identified as a problem and dealt with. The result was the beginning of the Legal Matrix.

We also reflect upon the early 60's when America appeared to be in a cultural renaissance. It was a time when Americans were expressing themselves in new ways. There was free love, free sex and overall discovery. Additionally, and very important to American development, during this time there were great movements in the area of civil rights. It was during this time that critical parts of the Legal Matrix were being developed to discourage those precise types of activity.

The Definition of Chaos:

A closer look at the state of chaos shows us that chaos is borne out of the uninhibited pursuit of happiness. A pursuit of ones desires at all costs and without regard to anyone else or their feelings. The results of chaos are destruction and fear. Again, modern day Iraq is an example of chaos. In Iraq there is constant destruction and fear. However, we know that America, which has interest in oil and other resources, will not allow that state to exist. The same goes for the drug industry that exists in the inner cities across this country. There are many black and brown men and women making large amounts of money by selling drugs. At the same time, these people are putting their own rules and regulations in place to govern the drug industry. America considers this activity a chaotic state and has created laws to suppress, control, and destroy the industry.

Chaos today does not exist on the same level as in ancient times. Today, chaotic states are isolated and exist not as a part of the Legal Matrix but outside of the law. Outside the law refers to glitches in the Legal Matrix or programs not acting as they should. As we know, all glitches in the system must be dealt with or terminated. For instance we all have the constitutional right to bear arms. Some states allow for carrying a concealed weapon while

14

others do not. Either way, any activity with a gun that is not outlined and allowed by the Legal Matrix is an act outside the law and that activity will be dealt with by the law.

Chaotic states are normally associated with criminal enterprises whether small or large scale. But whether large or small, chaos, destruction and confusion creates an unhealthy environment and thereby an unhealthy life. Prolonged existence is either impossible or utterly miserable when there is chaos in our personal life or chaos in the Legal Matrix.

Personal Causes of chaos:

- Dimmed spirits
- Lack of expression
- Hopelessness
- Desperation
- Clouded reality

Dimmed spirits occur when individuals realize that life is not what they expected it to be. Often we can not put a finger on it, but we know that something is not right. We work everyday, but we are unfulfilled. We have families but they do not totally complete us. We just don't shine as bright as we are capable of shining.

Lack of expression is the knowledge that you have a desire on the inside that is not allowed to surface. Lack of expressive outlets will lead to claustrophobic feelings. We begin to think that we cannot be ourselves or reach our full potential.

Hopelessness is the feeling that for some reason, we can not be successful in the system in which we live (the environment, job or relationship), and that we can do nothing to change it.

Desperation is the anxiety that makes us act without regard to other people's rights or the consequences of our actions. It's a lack of future vision. When you can not see a future way out, desperation is the only choice.

Clouded Reality is when a person is living in a fantasy, an unhealthy fantasy. These people go through life without any concern of the world. These people exist in the shell of our families, our neighborhoods, and our limited knowledge. We are not productive in society because we can not come to grip with the world that exists outside our minds.

If we take these elements of chaos separately or together we find that people will conduct themselves in ways that will lead to their introduction to the Legal Matrix. For example, lack of expression, turning to dimmed spirits, leading to hopelessness, desperation and clouded reality causes people to become involved with the drug life. It does not matter where in the spectrum you exist, selling, casual user, or addict the drug life is a life of chaos. I understand it is not a universally excepted principle that drugs lead to chaos and destruction. There are many people who fight for the legalization of certain drugs and they would surely disagree with me. As it stands today, the drug life is chaotic, if for no other reason than because it is illegal.

The drug life entails the illusion of pleasure. It leads to having thoughts of receiving pleasure from selling drugs; the perceived benefits and illusory success that comes from selling the drugs. Additionally there is the illusion of pleasure, satisfaction, peace, or happiness from the use of drugs. Nevertheless, the drug life is a form of Chaos. The dealers, distributors and manufactures are constantly on the edge, wondering when they will get caught or killed in the industry. Those involved in the use of drugs are waiting for the end, which is rock bottom, jail, or death.

Considering it a chaotic state, the Legal Matrix has created specific programs to deal with it.

The drug life is just one example of a chaotic state. There are many other ways to create a chaotic environment. In order to deal with the chaos, the Legal Matrix has created order. Despite the existence of chaos, the pleasant reality is that the Legal Matrix was designed to create order and give us the opportunity to be successful. I submit that the offerings of the Legal Matrix itself are not enough. To be truly successful and at peace, you must know the Legal Matrix. By knowing the Legal Matrix, you must understand that at the opposite end of the benefits of the Legal Matrix is the fact that it can also imprison us. In fact, it imprisons millions of people in this country. The imprisonment of the Legal Matrix even goes beyond the penal institutions. As the Legal Matrix has evolved into its current state it imprisons people in various ways - slavery, mental destruction, environmental and communal situations.

Because of the fear of chaos, the Legal Matrix set out to create order and control.

Order

Chaos must be controlled, therefore order must exist. Most of us can agree that true peace comes from order, not chaos. The Legal Matrix was created to sustain order. As exemplified by the current state of Iraq, historic riots in American prisons, the riots in the streets during the civil rights era, and the Rodney King decision, the need for order in our society is absolute. We must embrace order, or at least the concept that order must exist. Without order people would do whatever pleases them. Even for the die heart revolutionary, who likes to challenge the system, we all understand that order gives standards that help us survive.

Order helps us while we are driving through an intersection, walking down the street, pursuing a degree in college. Even the way that night, day, and the movement of the seasons help sustain our lives. There is no doubt that order gives us structure and reliability.

The Necessity of Order

Order protects us from harm. It gives us remedies when we have been violated and gives us a means to employ and pursue justice. In this country, it did not take the government long to determine that chaos was not going to be tolerated. Laws were made, or shall I say revised because we know that even before the first settlers came to the country bringing with them laws and regulations from Europe, the American Indians had a concept of order that sustained life in this land.

The only reason that there was a time of chaos and even now, pockets of chaos, is due to the citizenry stretching or testing of the laws that currently exist. Americans from the beginning have been known to stretch and challenge systems. The United States government soon became aware that in order to establish peace and prosperity in this country there was a necessity for complete order. The hard part was to determine exactly how to impose the order upon the United States citizens, especially those who felt that the Declaration of Independence provided the right to live life in pursuit of happiness without restraint from the government.

At various points in history, the concept of individualized rights was challenged by the government's vision for order. Accordingly the courts and tribunals began to shape and define the Constitution and interpret its privileges and benefits.

Part of the necessity of Order is to provide balance in the Legal Matrix. By design or by coincidence, there is a balance in the Legal Matrix. The balance is between the pursuit of success and happiness by individual citizens and the goals of the system itself. We want freedom and the Legal Matrix wants control.

Order = the Legal Matrix = Control

A dictionary definition states that Matrix is an environment or the material in which something develops. The system that underlines our everyday lives is neither good nor bad, it just is. The purpose of the Legal Matrix is to control us. There is no escaping the Legal Matrix. As we discussed the Legal Matrix has developed over time through various governmental measures to ensure that chaos would be controlled. In America specifically, the system itself is constantly evolving and changing. Take, for instance, the process of identification in America. There was strong opposition to creating a national identification system. Historically, the motivation for such a system was to be able to properly identify and account for each American. Many years ago the idea of the identification system started with America's desire to control the increased immigration of Chinese people on American soil. Attempts to keep the Chinese from over populating American soil took many forms and thus began the public push for the nation identification system.

Today, our lives are affected by the internet culture. The Computer has created an ease of ability to monitor our everyday lives. The Patriot Act has been used in ways that extend beyond terrorism and into regular crime detection and prosecution. This is evidence that the Legal Matrix is working full steam ahead at gaining ways to control our existence.

In our personal lives, purpose is what guides us, what motivates us, and that which keeps us full and healthy. Our purpose in life can be generally described as the pursuit of individual peace and happiness. This can be translated into the ability to pursue our individual goals, even if they involve a greater societal good, and the goal to live our lives according to our personal definition of success. Some people would cringe at the thought that individualism should be a purpose of mankind. We are told and taught that life is about relationships[ii], so logically it would seem that our purpose should also be focused on relationships. On the contrary, it is the individual who must be complete before any union can be complete; accordingly, our purpose is correctly focused on the individual first.

Beyond the individualistic purpose, I submit to you, that by reading this book we are introduced to a new purpose. Our purpose is to understand the Legal Matrix so that we will be equipped to achieve peace, happiness and all other goals that we set for ourselves. We must clearly understand that we can not truly achieve our goals or live a successful life unless we become aware of the Legal Matrix and learn how to live with the system. Some of us have learned the Legal Matrix by chance, experience or by teaching. Regardless of the source of knowledge, no one in this country will be truly successful if they can not live within the Legal Matrix – this is our purpose.

The Legal Matrix was created to eliminate the chaos. The Legal Matrix has proven to be very effective at this cause, but it has come at a cost to all of us. Every day we are at risk of losing our liberty to the Legal Matrix. Every day we are exposed to possible harassment based on the Legal Matrix. To create an environment void of chaos and to gain control, it was necessary to create the Legal Matrix.

The primary purpose of the Legal Matrix was, and is, to establish order from chaos. Some would say that the purpose of the Legal Matrix is to advance America's selfish power goal, like the goal to become or maintain the status as the strongest nation. There is a difference however between the desire to maintain order and the quest for power. Under the surface, the Legal Matrix is without a doubt a quest for power, but the main goal, the main purpose, is to establish order and control.

Chapter II

Who's In Control? How Police, Prosecutors & Judges Affect the Legal Matrix

The Legal Matrix controls every aspect of our lives. Everything around us, every hour of the day, and every minute of the hour is controlled by the Legal Matrix. This control is played out through the laws (programs) that govern us. Everything in our life has a legal aspect. Think about it. There is nothing we do or want to do that does not have a legal consequence. From opening a business, taking care of your child, your relationship with other people, to your travel in the city and country, everything has a legal aspect. So when people ask what the Legal Matrix is, I respond, "It is everything and all things around us."

Control - What is it?

When people mess up, they become a part of the Matrix as they become a problem that must be solved. Accordingly, they must be dealt with, destroyed, or controlled. Simply put, control is the ability of the system, the Legal Matrix, to put you in jail in a split second, to get rid of you. Now, if that is not control, I don't know what is.

Many people talk about control. I have often heard the argument that "the system" controls our lives and that we really have no control at all. I consider that argument to be very pessimistic, but the argument does have merit when we look at life through the code of the Legal Matrix. To the people who feel as though there is no control, I want to offer a different view. There was a time when I thought all control was in the hands of government, but it is not intended to be that way. The government is supposed to work for the people and on the behalf of the people. More importantly, we, the citizens, are the ones who should guide the decisions of our government. We elect officials so they can write laws on our behalf. Whether or not we utilize our ability, by being vocal and voting, we have the opportunity to be involved in the process. The problem is that too many people choose not to be involved. We sit back and complain about the system, instead of acting for its betterment. If we get involved in the political process, we will have more "Oracles." (resources that help us achieve our goals) working on our behalf and less "Agents" (people who work for the system) trying to put us under the system.

Sean "P. Diddy" Combs, Rap Mogul and visionary discussed the possibility of change during his "Citizen Change" campaign. He believes that if the "hip hop generation" (defined as the 17-35 year old demographic) got more involved in politics, the financial and vocal power of this demographic could turn America on its back. A way to transfer the control of the Legal Matrix or at least to force it to recognize our voice is to get involved with the process.

Regardless of the intent, the Legal Matrix does not have absolute control. Even if it is true that there is no absolute control, each individual does control the most important resource in the world - the knowledge that we have in our mind (of course, this does not take into account the medications, some voluntary, others induced, that will cause us to think out of our normal mind and fail to use our full mental capacity). Medication and drugs aside, we have the greatest tool of all of mankind - the mind. No one can take it away from us. If we have our mind and imagination intact, nothing can stop our progress. There is no greater control than that which we have over our mind. So dispel the myth that the system or the Legal Matrix is in control, despite the Legal Matrix's power to crush and destroy us physically or to damage our spirits, we can use our mind, the only tool to help us get out of the slumps, to help us stay out of trouble and succeed in our lives.

If no one can control our minds, how can others control our destiny? Many times this control is gained through our relationship choices.

Control goes hand in hand with relationships. Our entire existence involves relationships, relationships with people, places and things. Through use of our minds we have the ability to control our relationships so that our travel and existence within the Legal Matrix is a smooth one.

Relationships We Can Control:

♦ Family
♦ Friends
♦ Spiritual
♦ Employment
♦ Financial

The relationship often determines the type of control. The relational environment of the Legal Matrix is very important because relationships will determine your position within the Legal Matrix. For instance, the people you surround yourself with are important to your success and ability to navigate safely through the Legal Matrix.

> The person you decide to have a child with, marry or have a relationship with will affect your life in the Legal Matrix.

Similarly, relationships that you may or may not have with people who are directly a part of the Legal Matrix will affect the way you go through the system. Within the Legal Matrix, good relationships lead to good results. Kind of like the old boy network, the people whom you know can play a major part in your navigation through the Legal Matrix and through life.

Our personal relationships are very important to our ability to live in the Legal Matrix. If we are careful about our relationships, then we will better prepare ourselves for life in the Legal Matrix. The person you decide to have a child with, marry or have a relationship with will affect your life in the Legal Matrix. These choices lead to other major life changing decisions, like determining if you will go through child custody issues, child support issues, divorce, violence (domestic or otherwise). The possibilities are endless. Relationships are one of the primary reasons we end up effected by the Legal Matrix - friends, influences, pressures are all entries into the Legal Matrix. Control of our relationships lead to the ability to control our lives.

Who is in control?

"If there is any fixed star in our constellation, it is that no official, high or petty, can prescribe what shall be orthodox in politics, nationalism, religion, or other matters of opinion or force citizens to confess by word or act their faith therein."

- Supreme Court Justice Robert Jackson in West Virginia State Board of Education v. Barnette

So who is in control? This is a really loaded question. You control your destiny, but the Legal Matrix controls your existence. That sounds conflicting, but it's true. You have the ability to make certain decisions about your life, your goals and your desires. You can choose your profession, your relationships, and your activities. You do not control your existence. You do not control the speed limit, the rules in public places, what you can do in your relationships (you can not act with violence to control anyone, not even your child) nor much else in the outside environment. So there is a balance of control. It's sort of like a seesaw. Similar to the scales of justice but the scale normally tips in favor of the system – the Legal Matrix. Sometimes you have the upper angle where your decisions appear to be supreme. Other times you have the lower angle where you feel that you can not do anything but obey the laws that "hold you down."

Control is an important subject because we control our minds. We are able to make decisions that will have a lasting effect on how we navigate through the Legal Matrix. Control your mind, don't sit back and let the system control it for you. Don't take everything, or for that matter, anything at face value. Investigate and make a determination on your own.

26

The Matrix movie posed that precise question about control. From all indications it has been revealed that the Legal Matrix wants to control us, our desires and our emotions. It is up to us to recognize this and set the limits. We have the choice, we can either be totally dominated by the Legal Matrix, or we can learn how to work within the system. So regardless of the Legal Matrix and its purpose, true control lies with each of us.

The controller of the Legal Matrix is not easily identified. In fact who or what is in control is a futile debate and looking for its discovery would be for those who have time to burn. The system exists regardless of the person we may think is in control. One of the benefits of our democracy and this form of government around the world is that the system will survive regardless of who is in power at any specific time.

So to visualize the control system of the Legal Matrix, we can use *The Matrix* movie. In the movie, the machines controlled the system. We never saw the lead machine or the origination of the machines; we were just told how they came about. Further, we saw that Agents in the movie were the face of the system. The Agents were used to effectuate the Matrix and its design. Similarly, there is no exact face of the Legal Matrix. We do know that there are various Agents who keep the system going, who effectuate the desires of the system; those are the police officers, prosecutors, legislators and others.

To show that the Legal Matrix is a system based on control and that everyone is subject to its control, Look at Amber McClenny the 21 year old in the 343rd Quartermaster Company stationed in Iraq was among the members who refused to carry out a mission with unarmored vehicles. Her punishment was less pay, having to work the hours of 8 am to 10 pm seven days a week for 30 days, all because she was concerned about her own safety over that of the Legal Matrix.

Just as in the movie, Neo, Morpheous, and the crew were part of the civilization fighting to defeat or at least overcome the Matrix. The same holds true for the Legal Matrix. All of us as United States citizens are in a constant battle to ensure that the Legal Matrix does not take away our rights and privileges. We are attempting to exist with the system and establish some type of harmony with it. This book is the guideline for establishing such harmony.

Now let's discuss the pieces of the Legal Matrix puzzle.

The Agents

In *The Matrix* movie, the Agents were the people who put into effect the inner workings or rules of the Matrix itself. In our lives, an Agent is a tool of the Legal Matrix. An Agent is a person who works for the benefit of the Legal Matrix's purpose – we previously defined that purpose as order and control. Examples of Agents are the United States Attorney General, your local prosecutor, many of the police and law enforcement officers, judges and even politicians. Most importantly, any person who is able to take away your freedom or liberty is an Agent.

The Legal Matrix's entire existence rests on the ability of the Agents to keep the system going. The Legal Matrix would not exist without the use of Agents to draft, apply and enforce the goals of the Legal Matrix. There are good Agents and bad Agents, and sometimes, whether you believe it or not, we may become Agents.

Definition of a "Good Agent": The good Agents are in the Legal Matrix but not of the Legal Matrix, meaning they work within the system but help fight to ensure our rights are not violated. Examples are the court administrators, good politicians and other people who work for the government.

Definition of a "Bad Agent": The bad Agents are the people who have become so involved in the Legal Matrix that they are instrumental in turning a blind eye to injustice and our civil liberties. They work to violate our rights, and they are good at it.

Sometimes, ordinary people like you and I become Agents. We become Agents when we perform jury duty, when we work for a government employer or when we call the police to assist us or to intervene in a personal situation. It's at these times that the most disconnected, everyday, average citizen can play the part of an Agent. An example of our participation as an Agent is when we act as jurors for a judicial proceeding. As a juror, we are given the unique ability to judge another and determine another's guilt or innocence. Ultimately, jurors are in the position to put someone in jail or give them freedom. This is a time when our peers are supposedly the deciders of fact. But in reality, juries are often influenced, sometimes played and other times overturned by bigger Agents - the Court of Appeals.

The worst part about the agent participation of a juror is the fact that many people try hard to avoid jury duty. I have been in several trials where I hoped that there were more African Americans on the jury. Instead, the few that were in the jury pool gave the judge several excuses as to why they could not sit for the jury. Now if these people were on the other side of the coin and they were facing prison, I am sure they would want to have a jury of their peers and at least a few people on the jury that looks like them.

Agents of the Legal Matrix are the people that we must respect and fear. We respect the Agents because of their ability to influence our lives. We fear the Agents for those same reasons; again these are the people who can take away our liberties and freedoms. The Agents help create the laws that affect us everyday and they direct our exposure and awareness of the Legal Matrix by bringing criminal and other charges against us. Don't get me wrong. I hold fast to the assertion that Agents in the Legal Matrix work very hard and they should be commended and respected for their dedication. I too call the police when I am in trouble, I too think about suing a person when I have been wronged, so I must admit that the Legal Matrix works to my benefit. However, we fear the Agents for the same reasons that we respect them - their ability to affect our lives.

Agents don't make the Legal Matrix they just work it.

Whether they know it or not, Agents are expendable. Realistically speaking, as we learned, the U.S. Government must maintain some of type of systematic organization, order and control so it is understandable that the Legal Matrix continues to exist. Why? Because order is necessary. Though the Agents help run the Legal Matrix, the existence of the Legal Matrix is bigger than and beyond the control of the Agents that are actually a part of the system. No matter how hard the Agent works, no matter how dedicated the Agent is, the Legal Matrix will go on if and/or when the particular Agent gets caught in the Legal Matrix themselves (everyday we witness elected officials getting indicted for criminal violations) or cease to exist.

Even when a U.S. President or any government official is replaced with another, the system continues to roll. It does not matter if the Agents are Black or White, democrat or republican the system utilizes everything and everyone to achieve its purpose and ensure its survival. The truth of the matter is that regardless of who the Agent is the system controls our destiny. We will have laws that we must adhere to or we will be dealt with.

We fear the Agents based on the fact that power is intoxicating and it causes people to act in selfish ways. Things and activities that were once done for the benefit of all people become clouded by the drive for personal gain. It is at this time, when greed and the lust for power take over, that we must fear Agents the most. I was recently involved in a nationally recognized murder trial. My client was a high school football star, nationally ranked, who found himself caught in the Legal Matrix. He was charged with murder based on the following facts:

My client and his two friends attempted to rob a drug dealer in their community. They attempted this robbery with toy guns. What they did not expect or know was that the person they were going to rob had a real gun. When the boys approached the person's vehicle, he began shooting. He killed one of the three friends. In Ohio there is a law that allows a person to be charged with murder, when that person was committing a felony act and someone is killed. This law sounds like a law school exam question. So under this legal fiction my client was charged with the death of his friend, when in fact another person was the one who pulled the trigger and killed the young boy.

Now this case shows that 1) the programs (the laws) in the Legal Matrix are often very serious and potentially very severe and 2) the Agents in the Legal Matrix can sometimes be very heartless. I say this because the prosecutor's office had the choice of charging my client, a young high school football star, with murder, or they had the option of charging the trigger man and charging my client with what he actually did – attempt a robbery. The difference was jail or freedom.

Brilliantly, the legal team I was involved with was able to negotiate the charges down and an equally brilliant and courageous judge decided not to send these young men to jail and give them a second chance at life. [iii]

When the drive of an Agent is power and control, the decisions they make may inflict long term damage in our lives, while the Agent is trying to accomplish short term concerns and goals. A prime example is the reduction of our civil liberties in an effort to fight the war

> The problem is not the Agents but our ignorance of the system.

on terror. We should be mindful of giving up our long term rights and protections under the constitution.

In *The Matrix* movie, the enemy was the system itself while the enforcers were called the "Agents" In the Legal Matrix there are many "Agents" with various titles and positions of power to enforce the laws and affect our lives. The problem is not the Agents but our ignorance of the system. To often, activists, educators and others preoccupy their time with concern over the "Agents," who they are, where they are from and who they are working for. That is not our concern. That is not the problem. Don't worry about the Agents, instead focus on the system and the way to work within it, navigate through it and maybe change it.

Who are the Agents?

As we know, the Legal Matrix is about control. The Legal Matrix is all around us. On the surface the Agents are the people who work on behalf of the Legal Matrix, ensuring that the Legal Matrix achieves its purpose. The Agents are the people who run the Legal Matrix. They are the ones sent or hired to keep the programs in order. It's important for you to understand that there are both good and bad Agents. Agents can be identified as police officers, prosecutors, judges, probation officers or any person with the authority to take away our freedoms and our liberty.

Agents are a force of the Legal Matrix but not all of the Agents realize their part in the overall system. For instance, some prosecutors working in the federal and state systems go about their daily routines without regard to the lives that are being affected by their work. Sometimes the Agents are not fully cognizant of how their actions affect the lives of innocent people. Furthermore, these same Agents don't realize that the moment they walk outside the confines of the programs, they too will be affected by the Legal Matrix. In other words, the moment an Agent acts out of character, that Agent will be punished. Take for example, Oliver North, the former United States military official who was ultimately accused of supporting American enemies through the sell of arms (or at least turning a blind eye to the conduct) and how he was hung out to dry by the administration that initially supported him. Once the mess hit the fan, he was abandoned. Logically, if he was involved in some type of wrongdoing while working for the government, others were aware of his conduct and may have even supported it, but he alone was blamed.

Agents Identified - The Law Enforcement Officers

It should go without saying that law enforcement officers are a key component to the Legal Matrix. They investigate, pursue and solve crimes. We will discuss the officers in detail, but it is sufficient to say that without law enforcement officers there would be no control and the Legal Matrix would not exist.

Agents Identified - The Grand Juries

The grand jury system is a major Agent in the Legal Matrix. The grand jury consists of a group of citizens who are summoned to hear prosecutors' present information to support the bringing of criminal charges against individuals.

Many cases in the United States and its territories begin as an indictment from a grand jury. Whether the crime is considered a federal or state violation, the grand jury process is a staple in our American legal system. The process is suppose to provide a way to anonymously and fairly review a particular set of evidence against an accused person to see if it is possible that the person committed a crime. Now I am being very careful with my word choice. The grand juries

> In this Legal environment, it's easy to accuse and indict anyone for a crime.

do not determine if there is enough evidence to prove a case against a particular person or group. That is, to ultimately prove their guilt. Instead, the standard is whether enough evidence exists for the grand jury to agree that a crime likely took place and that the person being charged is the likely responsible party.

It has been said that some grand juries will indict a ham sandwich. There was a recent situation in Cuyahoga County, Ohio where a judge told the grand jury that they could not present an indictment unless they agreed that the person accused could be found guilty of the accused act. This statement sparked a serious legal battle between the county prosecutor's office and the judge. In fact, the dispute made its way to the Ohio Supreme Court which ordered the judge to change his language to comport with the probability standard. Despite the decision of the Ohio Supreme Court, I can see where the Cuyahoga County Judge was coming from. It would seem that, before you put anyone through the turmoil and embarrassment of legal charges, the grand jury should be charged with the responsibility to review the evidence to see if there is enough to decide that the person could be found guilty. That's not too much to ask of our legal system, but obviously, the Agents would not have it that way.

To see how the grand jury system works, we only need to look at a decision by the highest court in the land. In *U.S. v. Dionisio*,[iv] the Supreme Court held that Federal Grand Juries may freely use investigative techniques without any preliminary showing of reasonableness to justify exercise of these powers. This means that a prosecutor can attempt to get an indictment against a particular person by any means necessary. They can use investigative techniques that would not be admissible in the trial itself. They can use hearsay[v] and they do not have to present evidence of innocence *U.S. v. Williams*[vi]. These decisions informally designated the Federal Grand Jury as a tool of the prosecutor with a license to present all types of reliable and even unreliable information about an accused person. This means the evidence can be incomplete or very little.   If the prosecutors' purpose is not served – a paper indictment that officially charges a person with a crime - they can even get rid of that specific grand jury and present the case to a different grand jury, thereby starting the process all over again. Then we wonder why there are so many cases and the criminal system is so clogged up!

The federal grand jury process has many faults, and needs to be overhauled to eliminate these faults. Some of the important ones are:

1. **A grand jury target (or person who is probably going to be indicted) has no right to appear before the grand jury and tell the jurors, under oath, the events which took place from the target's standpoint.**

If a grand jury were allowed to hear the story from the target's standpoint, the grand jury might be less willing to indict. Under New York law, a target has the right to testify before the grand jury. Under federal law, the prosecutor has the right to determine whether he will permit a willing target to testify to try to persuade the grand jury not to indict him or her.[vii]

2. **The grand jury process is not supervised by the court, any governmental organization, or by the prosecutor's own employer, the Justice Department.** Many federal judges have told me that they have no control over what takes place before the grand jury. The prosecutor uses the grand jury as he/she would deal with an array of manikins. The prosecutor

creates a paper record by making statements to the court reporter (which are overheard by such members of the grand jury who happened to show up for the session), and introduces documentary or physical exhibits into the same record, and finally presents a piece of paper (the form for an indictment) to be signed by the grand jury foreperson so the grand jury can go back to their jobs or homes. Because the grand-jury system is so one-sided, it is a no-brainer for the members. What else can they do?

3. **The grand-jury proceedings are held in secret, in accordance with a federal rule which requires each grand-jury investigation to be conducted in secret.** A Knowing violation of Rule 6 may be punished as a contempt of court. This requirement enables the prosecutors to act in secret and leave no discoverable trail for aggrieved persons and the public to hold federal prosecutors accountable for wrongdoing, unless they can somehow break the secrecy requirement. Of course, the secrecy requirement never stops prosecutors from leaking secret information to the press, particularly through formal press releases, to be able to publicize their secret proceedings and poison the jury pool.

In our pursuit to understand the inner workings of the Legal Matrix, we a deeper look at some of the Justice Department's grand jury rules.

9-11.232 Use of Hearsay in a Grand Jury Proceeding

As a general rule, it is proper to present hearsay to the grand jury, *United States v. Calandra.*[viii] Each United States Attorney should be assured that hearsay evidence presented to the grand jury will be presented on its merits so that the jurors are not misled into believing that the witness is giving his or her personal account. *See United States v. Leibowitz;*[ix] *but see United States v. Trass.*[x]

9-11.233 Presentation of Exculpatory Evidence (evidence that the accused is not guilty of the crime).

In *United States v. Williams,*[xi] the Supreme Court held that the Federal courts' supervisory powers over the grand jury did not include the power to make a rule allowing the dismissal of an otherwise valid indictment where the prosecutor failed to introduce substantial exculpatory evidence to a grand jury. It is the policy of the Department of Justice, however, that when a prosecutor conducting a grand jury inquiry is personally aware of substantial evidence that directly negates the guilt of a subject of the investigation the prosecutor must present or otherwise disclose such evidence to the grand jury before seeking an indictment against such a person. While a failure to follow the Department's policy should not result in dismissal of an indictment, appellate courts may refer violations of the policy to the Office of Professional Responsibility for review.

With our legal system reliant on the grand jury system, we are guaranteed that prosecutors will be able to get all the indictments they seek, and defense attorneys will be forced to save innocent people from the Legal Matrix. We know this is not a problem of the future but a current dilemma. Statistics show that in every jurisdiction, indictments are up with thousands of people being caught in the Legal Matrix even when the evidence against them is weak or nonexistent.

Agents Identified - The Prosecutors

Prosecutors wield enormous power. Through the use of the grand juries, prosecutors are able to make unlimited demands for documents and evidence. They can subpoena unwilling witnesses and work immunity deals all in the effort to bring a formal complaint against the subject, in other words to prosecute.

The prosecutors decide whether to charge an individual for a crime and how serious that charge should be. They decide whether to take a case to trial or to offer a plea bargain to avoid trial. With power comes duty. Prosecutors have the duty to seek "truth" and thereby disclose to the defense any information that could help prove a person's innocence. This pursuit of "truth" does not happen as often as it should.

> Prosecutors are often vilified as a major problem in the fight for freedom from the Legal Matrix. We love them when they are working for us and hate them when we are on the receiving end of an indictment.

Prosecutors are often vilified as a major problem in the fight for freedom from the Legal Matrix. We love them when they are working for us and hate them when we are on the receiving end of an indictment. I remember times in trial where I wanted to walk over to the prosecutors table and "pop" the guy in the head. I, like many

defense attorneys, get frustrated because I know that they use
unfair tactics and strategies to get their convictions (I will discus
this subject more lately).   But as we learned earlier, there are good
and bad Agents.   There are some prosecutors who work for justice
and it happens more often than we think.

I had the pleasure of meeting and working with a
supervising prosecutor in the Cuyahoga County Prosecutor's
Office, who took the position that he was not out to put innocent
people in jail. He and I spent a lot of time discussing the legal
system, the disparities, the acts of injustice by prosecutors and the
fact that people/defendant don't get a fair shake in this system.
More importantly, I was able to put his talk to the test when I
represented a young man whom was not guilty as charged and the
prosecutor's evidence against him was very weak. This prosecutor
had the opportunity and actually took the time to review the facts
of the case and then help get a dismissal of the charges against my
client.   The Agent Prosecutor is on the front line of the Legal
Matrix's control plans, approach them with caution and be
prepared to fight.

Agents Identified - The Judge

Judges are part of the Legal Matrix. They are a mixed bag
of Agents, some good and others not so good, others just plain bad.
The bad Agents are easily identified in the courtrooms across this
country.   They rule with discrimination and profiling opinions.
They are the judges who bring personal feelings and attitudes into
the courtroom making the experience a nightmare for the
defendant and his attorney. In some situations, judges hand down
sentences that are unfair. One such example happened where a
young Black woman was charged with her first Driving Under the
Influence charge. Her situation was a tragic one, where she killed
two innocent people traveling on a highway. Her sentence for this
event, her first criminal act in her life, was 20 years in prison. For
the same act, in a courtroom in the same building, a Caucasian man

received a 6 year sentence for the same crime – a DUI causing the death of two innocent people. Now tell me where is the justice when two similarly situated people, differing mainly in the color of their skin, can get two extremely different sentences. The answer is that there are good Agents and bad Agents, so beware.

I had the opportunity to speak with an attorney, Rufus Sims, a veteran in the game. He was disturbed because a common pleas judge, while at a pre-trial, announced a bond hearing out of the blue. At this hearing, she raised a bond for his client from $5000 surety, from which the defendant had posted a bond and was released, to a $25,000 cash bond. Now historically, the reason for bond is to ensure that the defendant will show up for trial and that he is not a risk to the community. In this case, the defendant was always present at the pre-trials and never indicated that he would flee. More importantly he had no criminal record and was not a risk to the community. The judge indicated to the attorney that she reviewed the facts and independently decided to raise the bond. That is injustice, more pointedly, that is the Legal Matrix in full effect. It's the system working to keep us in control and Agents who lose work to keep the screws of the system working. So how does that make a seasoned attorney look - terrible, he now has to deal with a damaged reputation and the client is forced to develop his defense from behind bars when he was legally out of jail?

Tools of the Judge – Judicial Sentencing

Sentencing is a very important part of the judges ability to act in his or her capacity. The rational part of the Legal Matrix, the good Agents, found that too many judges were making decisions based on judgments of the individual characteristics of the alleged criminals or even plain prejudice. The system wanted to ensure more consistent sentencing. For the most part, the ability to make sentencing decisions rests in the area of judicial discretion. Now to me that seem like a logical way to sentence an individual, based on that individual's personal characteristics in relation to the crime committed. The Legal Matrix wanted more control, so the Federal Sentencing Guidelines were created. These guidelines will be discussed later in the text with an example of its power demonstrated.

A Look at Average Sentences in Specific Cases[xii]:

Offenses and Penalties in months:	
Drug trafficking	82.3
Sexual Abuse	73.3
Assault	38.8
Manslaughter	34.2
Bribery	22.9

The Problem with Sentencing: A Good Judicial Agent: Supreme Court Justice William Rehnquist.

> So, not only did the Legal Matrix take away the judges ability to use his or her discretion before taking away a person's liberty and putting someone in jail, but now, the judges that dare to use discretion will be cataloged and then reviewed by the federal government - the Legal Matrix.

A Judicial Agent on the good side is the Chief Justice of the United States Supreme Court, William Rehnquist, who scolded Congress for not consulting with the judiciary before enacting legislation that limits a judge's ability to impose lighter sentences within the federal guideline and the stripping of a judge's ability to use discretion. The anti-crime bill passed by Congress and signed into law by President Bush in April 2003 and sponsored by Republican Tom Feeney of Florida, supported by Attorney General John Ashcroft, reduced federal judges' discretion in sentencing criminals and required reports to Congress on any judge who departs from the sentencing guidelines. Judge Rehnquist said that this cataloging of the judges based on their decision to utilize judicial discretion before sentencing a person is "troubling" and could appear to be an unwarranted and ill-considered effort to intimidate individual judges in the performance of their judicial duties." Mary Cheh, a law professor at George Washington University, said that, "the sentencing process is even more removed from the judge …..and placed more heavily in the hands of prosecutors."[xiii] Some of the Judges, good Agents, have resigned from their positions because of these new laws. So, not only did the Legal Matrix take away the judges ability to use his or her discretion before taking away a person's liberty and putting someone in jail, but now the judges that dare to use discretion will be cataloged and then reviewed by the federal government - the Legal Matrix.

In a groundbreaking move, in the spring of 2005, the United States Supreme Court ruled that in order to hand down a maximum sentence of a crime, a jury must determine the facts that would lead to such a decision. Moreover, the court said that the sentencing guidelines were advisory, meaning that the guidelines are the guide but not the rule the judges must follow.

Tools of the Agent – One Bad Judicial Decision

Judges control the Legal Matrix by the way they decide legal questions. The judge is the gateway to jail or freedom. On the other hand, there are decisions by judges that extend the powers of the Legal Matrix. The overall effects of certain decisions clearly identify some judges as bad Agents. Take for instance the 2003 decision by

> Every mother and father must tell their children, especially in the inner cities of this country, not to ride in a car with anyone because if that person happens to have drugs or illegal materials in their possession, your child will be charged with a crime.

the U.S. Supreme Court in the case of *Maryland v. Pringle*[xiv]. In *Pringle* a passenger vehicle was stopped for speeding. The officer searched the vehicle and found $763 in cash in the glove compartment and five glassine baggies of cocaine from the back-seat armrest and the back seat. All three men in the vehicle denied ownership of the cocaine and the money and all three were arrested. Later while under arrest, one of the passengers – Pringle – waived his Miranda rights and admitted possession of the cocaine. He later tried to suppress this confession but the suppression attempt was denied in the trial court and caused the case to travel to the U.S. Supreme Court. The Supreme Court upheld the arrest by finding that all three occupants had knowledge of, and exercised dominion and control over the cocaine. Even though the cocaine was behind the armrest, one person was in the driver's seat, another in the passenger seat, and another in the back they were all able to be arrested and charged. Furthermore, the Court felt that a passenger is often engaged in a common enterprise with the driver and have the same interest in concealing the fruits or evidence of their wrongdoing.

So now, every mother and father must tell their children, especially in the inner cities of this country, not to ride in a car with anyone because if that person happens to have drugs or illegal materials in their possession, your child will be charged with a crime. The result of being charged with a crime is an experience with the Legal Matrix – getting interrogated, arrested, charged with a crime, forced to go to court, forced to defend yourself, the possibility of being convicted, dealing with jail and then dealing with post conviction release and a lifetime stigma. That is why it's important that we involve ourselves in the judicial selection process.

Question – Can Agents Be Trusted?

The Legal Matrix has a glitch that makes navigation of the system very difficult. This particular glitch is the abuse and corruption in the system that keeps the Legal Matrix operating – the corruption of the Agents. When the Agents don't play within the rules of the game, we are left with unpredictability that eventually leads to rebellion, revolt and destruction. There are many people in prison who were framed by the system. At the same time, there are individuals in prison who were fed up with the system and committed acts of violence out of frustration and hopelessness. In either example, the Agents worked against the citizens. Think about it, we can survive in this system, we

> There are many people in prison who were framed by the system. At the same time, there are individuals in prison who were fed up with the system and committed acts of violence out of frustration and

can be successful, but when Agents act out in corruption, the balance in the Legal Matrix is violently shifted and we are subject to fall from our level of control.

Although I acknowledge that there are honest police officers, prosecutors and judges, people of integrity who are the backbone of the system, I am aware that there is proof of corruption by the Agents in this country. As we can imagine, the corruption is deep. The drug war, in particular, creates many evils including corruption. Drugs tempt honest individuals to do things that they wouldn't normally do. When you add the fact that drugs have a street value that often rises into the millions of dollars, the temptation of corruption is very strong. When faced with the temptation to take, sell, trade, blackmail or use drugs, we can not trust the Agents in the legal Matrix, and that is just the beginning. Drugs tempt otherwise honest individuals to do things that they wouldn't normally do.

Police and Other Misconduct

Just look at some of the examples from around the country:

Georgia

- Marcus Lee Hall Jr., deputy sheriff of Jeff Davis County, pled guilty to distributing marijuana and faced a 5-year prison term. *Atlanta Constitution* May 22, 1993.

- **Ex-Sheriff** James Ronald Walker of Telfair County was arrested on charges of racketeering, extortion, illegal drugs and obstruction of justice after a state probe of his office, becoming the 28th Georgia Sheriff since 1981 indicted on criminal charges. Walker pleaded guilty to marijuana conspiracy charges in exchange for dropping cocaine trafficking charges. He admitted to taking payoffs to warn growers and dealers of surveillance. *Atlanta Constitution* August 18, 1993.

- **State prison guard** Roslyn Clark faced felony charges for selling cocaine out of her home. *Savannah News Press* April 19, 1993.

- Six Atlanta **police officers** were charged with stealing money during drug searches and taking bribes from drug dealers.

- Former Bleckley **county sheriff** Ed Coley was sentenced to 2 years for conspiracy to sell marijuana in order to raise enough money for an informant's defense on robbery charges. *Atlanta Constitution* April 27, 1994.

Michigan

- Detroit **police officers** James Harris and Angela Canoy were convicted on 17 counts of bribery, money laundering and narcotics possession. *Sturgis Journal* December 23, 1992.

- Detroit **police officer** Carl Webster was arrested with 15 pounds of cocaine when he was stopped for speeding in Texas. *Houston Chronicle* September 27, 1993.

New Mexico

- Albuquerque Corrections Officer Richard Rojo was arrested for selling cocaine to inmates in an undercover sting. *Albuquerque Tribune* May 5, 1993.

Nevada

- Reno **police officer** Gary Eubanks was arrested for selling amphetamines. *Reno Gazette* July 20, 1993.

New Jersey

- South Hackensack **Police Chief** Arthur Montenegro was arrested after accusations that he ordered one of his patrolmen not to file charges against 2 men busted for cocaine possession and for ordering the officer to falsify the arrest report and omit mention of the cocaine. *New York Times* February 3, 1994.

New York

- NYC **Detective** Joseph Simone, assigned to the elite NYPD-FBI Organized Crime Task Force, was arrested for passing sensitive information to the Victor J. Orena faction of the warring Colombia Mafia family. *New York Newsday* December 9, 1993.

- Four **corrections officers** at New York City's Rikers Island jail were arrested for smuggling cocaine to inmates in exchange for bribes. *New York Times* March 21, 1995.

- Ferman Jones, a decorated New York City officer assigned to a Brooklyn street **narcotics unit**, was convicted of conspiracy to distribute cocaine and heroin. *New York Newsday* April 6, 1995.

Oregon

- Portland Oregon **police officer** Bradley Benge was arrested for dealing marijuana seized in drug busts. *The Oregonian* March 4, 1995.

Pennsylvania

- John Sabatino, **ex-prosecutor** for Montgomery County PA, plead guilty to snorting drug evidence from his own case files. *Philadelphia Inquire* October 10, 1993.

- Impeachment proceedings were launched against **Pennsylvania Supreme Court Justice** Rolf Larsen after he was charged with 26 drug counts by a grand jury he had called to investigate colleagues on kickback charges. *New York Newsday* November 14, 1993.

Philadelphia

- Six Philadelphia **police officers** were convicted of conspiracy to violate civil rights and nearly 50 drug cases overturned, after revelations of illegal searches and falsified evidence. *Philadelphia Inquire* August 8, 1995.

San Diego

- A **House of Representatives** investigation into the corruption at the Customs Service accuses former San Diego Customs chief Alan Rappaport of aiding drug smugglers and preventing entry of intelligence on smugglers into a Customs computer system. *Dallas Morning News* June 12, 1995.

South Carolina

- Residents circulated a petition calling dissolution of the South Carolina town of City View after the third **police chief** in a month was arrested for marijuana trafficking. *Atlanta Constitution* February 9, 1995.

Texas

- **Deputies** of the federally funded narcotics task force Zavala County were indicted for skimming seized drugs and money. Dalla*s Morning News* July 21, 1995.

- **Police lieutenant,** Michael Siebe was arrested in connection with the disappearance of 350 pounds of cocaine from a police storehouse in Beaumont. *Dallas Morning News* June 17, 1994.

- Wise **County Sheriff** Leroy Eugene Burch was indicted on charges of conspiracy to extort tens of thousands of dollars from drug defendants and men wrongfully arrested for "sex crimes" at a local park. Burch faces a life term in prison. *Dallas Morning News* April 15, 1992.

- Former Nueces **County Sheriff** James T. Hickey was indicted for illegal use of drug forfeiture funds for a retroactive pay raise, office parties, and gifts to employees and his attorney, who also faces indictments. Hickey faces 10 years in prison. *Corpus Christi Caller Times* August 20, 1993.

Washington

- Roy B. Rutherford of Pierce County, WA, pleaded guilty to possession of marijuana and hashish. *Settle Times* November 18, 1993.

- 14 employees of Washington DC's Lorton Prison were arrested for conspiracy to provide cocaine, crack, heroin and money to inmates. *Seattle Times* November 7, 1993.

FBI Mail Order Scam

- Philadelphia **FBI agent** Kenneth Withers was arrested for running a mail-order business in which he peddled heroin stolen from FBI evidence lockers to dealers whose names he obtained from FBI files. *Knight-Ridder* June 6, 1994.

Noriegas Revenge

- Rene De La Cova, the **DEA agent** who arrested Manuel Noriega in the 1989 Panama Invasion, is on Administrative leave pending a DEA/IRS probe into charges that he diverted hundreds of thousands of dollars in under cover-operation drug money to a personal safe deposit box. *Seattle Times* November 4, 1993.

U.S. Government

- Dorothea Risenhoover, **former House of Representatives Post Office supervisor**, plead guilty to charges of cocaine possession and covering up embezzlement. She apparently cut a deal with a clerk to not rat on his skimming of the proceeds in exchange for him not telling on her for the coke he supplied. Wendell Magruder was charged with selling cocaine to House PO staff. *New York Newsday* May 20, 1992.

It was best stated when an FBI Director said that "it should be accepted as a fact that every police agency will uncover at least one instance of corruption within their ranks." For example, a 1997 survey of thirty-seven major city Police Departments in the United States revealed the arrest of 452 officers for felonies or misdemeanors. Furthermore, a major city Chief can expect, on average, to have ten officers charged with abuse of their police authority and five officers arrested for a felony. The FBI is not immune from the problem. "During the past two years, we had one agent convicted of embezzling government funds and another of espionage."[xv]

Police Misconduct in its Highest Form

The worst example of police corruption was reported in 2005 from the City of New York. Two retired New York City police detectives were charged by federal prosecutors with taking part in eight murders on behalf of the Mafia - most while one or both were still active members of the police force. One act in the indictment occurred in 1990 when the officers allegedly drove an unmarked police car, pulled over a Mafia captain on the Belt Parkway in Brooklyn and shot him to death for a rival mob figure. In another, in 1986, they flashed their badges and kidnapped a mobster, threw him in the trunk of their car and delivered him to a rival who tortured and killed him. The indictment says that the officers were on the payroll of the mob for years.[xvi]

Another example of police corruption occurred in 1994, in New Orleans, LA when federal agents arrested New Orleans police officer Len Davis for the contract killing of Kim Groves. On October 13, 1994, Kim Groves, a 32-year-old African-American mother of three, was assassinated for filing a brutality complaint against Officer Len Davis, who she had witnessed pistol-whipping a teenager. According to the New York Times, Officer Davis was taped giving a detailed description of Ms. Groves over his cellular phone. Soon after Ms. Groves was shot, the jubilant howl of "Yeah" and "Rock, rock-a-bye" was recorded over Officer Davis' phone. The FBI had already been monitoring Davis as a part of a drug investigation, where 30 cops had been charged with armed robbery, kidnapping, extortion, rape and murder over the past 3 years. Davis and 8 other officers were indicted on cocaine distribution charges after the FBI discovered they were protecting coke shipments at an abandoned dockside warehouse. "In the last three years, according to the December 19 New York Times, New Orleans cops have been charged with: "armed robbery, kidnapping, battery, bribery, extortion, rape, even murder; as many as 30 officers have been arrested, many of them convicted..."[xvii]

The fact that officer Len Davis was heading his own police force that participated in drug selling, domestic terrorism and even murder, leads to the question of how do we combat the Legal Matrix, or more importantly, how do we survive in the Legal Matrix when this type of corruption exists?

Even aside from outright police corruption, there are often ideas and tactics employed by police forces that ultimately cause more harm than good. For instance, in Fresno California, a paramilitary team of 20 to 30 submachine-gun wielding officers was created to fight the crime problems in that city. The SWAT team (SWAT means Special Weapons and Tactics) was created in December 1994, by then-Chief Ed Winchester, when Fresno was suffering from so much violent crime that some community leaders worried the city was on the verge of anarchy. The unit was designed to fight violent gun-toting criminals on their own turf.

They were considered America's most aggressive SWAT team. The team used military training and equipment to fight crime. But the SWAT team was only one of over 30,000 such teams in this country.

However, as would be expected, the unit found itself at the center of several high-profile lawsuits in its brief life. In two of the lawsuits, as Police Chief Jerry Dyer is quick to note, the city was exonerated. The unit was disbanded in December 21, 2001.

It should be no surprise that use of SWAT operations actually increases the violence by police officers against the targets. A few examples of violent SWAT operations will shed light on the problem. In Albuquerque New Mexico, a Navy SEAL trained SWAT team targeted a suspected drug dealer named Manuel Ramirez. In an attempt to capture him, one group of the team smashed through the back door while the other team members ripped off his front door with a tow truck. Ramirez was asleep on the couch and when the commotion started he reached for what was an unloaded gun, however, before he could get up he was shot dead. The raid produced marijuana cigarettes and a small amount of crystal methamphetamine.

In Greensboro, a SWAT team killed 56-year-old Charles Irwin Potts during an over-zealous narcotics raid. The team, in masks, kicked in his front door and as he jumped up from his card game, he was shot and killed. No drugs were found on the premises.

Police Perjury

Once legal proceedings begin the Legal Matrix forces us to deal with another type of police corruption, police perjury. Although perjury is against the law, it happens all the time. Frankly, there are not enough resources to prosecute everyone who commits perjury, because we all know that a guilty person would lie to avoid conviction or help themselves. I tell clients all the time that when the case boils down to your word vs. the officer's word, it is an uphill battle.

Despite our knowledge of perjury or lying, what would surprise most people and juries is the extent to which police officers lie on the stand. Often this is done to reinforce the prosecution of a case or to protect their standing within the law enforcement community. I have practiced in front of judges who know and admit that officers do lie on the stand, and many police officers have admitted to lying and having personal knowledge of their colleagues who lie on the stand.

Bad Police Work

As a defense attorney, my first thought was to use this section to attack the sometimes terrible investigative and undercover work of police officers. But the purpose of this text is not to attack anyone, but to inform everyone. The biggest glitch in the Legal Matrix occurs at the beginning of an investigation, the actual police work of investigating the crimes. I admit there are many officers who do fantastic jobs at investigating and uncovering crimes. On the other hand there are times when officers are not performing to the best of their ability. This failure to perform could be due to political pressures or other factors, but it happens.

One source of the pressure officers face is the high volume of violent crime that plagues every urban police department. Skilled detectives are few, and their caseloads are overwhelming. Too often, as a result of the above factors, police officers take the easy way out. Once they begin to suspect someone as the culprit, and this often occurs early in the investigation based on rather flimsy and circumstantial information, the investigation blindly focuses in on that adopted "target." Crucial pieces of evidence are overlooked and disregarded. Some witnesses are not interviewed, while others are seduced or coerced into telling the police what they want to hear.

An example of bad police work is the case involving Clarence Bradley, who was mentioned earlier. He was arrested in late August, four days after the crime was committed and on the weekend before school was to begin. The high school where the rape and murder took place was flooded with telephone calls by scared parents who refused to send their children to school until the murderer was caught. The arrest of Bradley calmed the community, and school started as scheduled. It was after Bradley's arrest that the investigators spent five hundred hours building the case against him. This is an example of the Legal Matrix working backward to achieve its purpose.

Well the story does not end there because, in addition to the police corruption, we also have to combat the prosecutorial misconduct.

Prosecutorial Misconduct

The primary duty of a prosecutor is to seek justice and to ensure that those who are guilty of crimes are brought to justice. Most law enforcement agents and government prosecutors subscribe to high professional standards of ethics and conduct. They take their work and their obligations very seriously. However, there are a small percentage of prosecutors who are increasingly subverting the standards of judicial fair play in their zeal to get convictions, to make a name for themselves and get promoted. They prosecute for self-serving purposes and often engage in outrageous misconduct.

In Cleveland, Ohio a talented prosecutor, a dazzling courtroom lawyer and minister, Aaron Phillips, reached the highest level of success when a local case he handled was broadcasted on Court TV. Phillips' closing argument was featured on national television. It was only a few days later when he was arrested for prosecutorial misconduct. He was accused of and eventually pled guilty to various charges including corruption and drug charges.

The event in Cleveland is not uncommon. There are about 30,000 local prosecutors in 2,341 jurisdictions. A recent study called "Harmful Error" a product of three years of research by The Center for Public Integrity, a private ethics watchdog group, found that since 1970, state and local prosecutors bent or broke the rules to help put 32 innocent people in prison, some under death sentence. This study was the first nationwide study of prosecutorial misconduct. Additionally, the study found that in more than 2,000 cases during that same period, appellate judges dismissed criminal charges, reversed convictions or reduced sentences based on prosecutorial misconduct. The study also revealed that of the 223 prosecutors around the nation who had been cited by judges, for two or more cases of unfair conduct only, two prosecutors had been disbarred in the past 33 years for mishandling criminal cases. In the construct of the Legal Matrix that news is not surprising. The Legal Matrix is about control, and what better way to control than the ability to imprison and monitor through the criminal justice system. So prosecutors will do whatever they need to do, sometimes employing questionable and illegal means, to accomplish their goals.

As noted by these examples, the misconduct must be addressed and it sometimes is. Take for instance that fact that the same study found 28 cases involving 32 defendants in which judges concluded that misconduct by prosecutors contributed to the convictions of innocent people. These 32 were later exonerated, 12 of them by use of DNA genetic evidence. Some of these innocent defendants had been convicted of murder, rape or kidnapping; some had been under death sentence before exoneration spared them. In 2,017 cases, appellate judges found misconduct serious enough to order dismissal of charges, reversal of convictions or reduction of sentences. In an additional 513 cases, at least one judge filing a separate concurring or dissenting opinion thought the misconduct warranted reversal.

> No practice is more ingrained in our criminal justice system than the practice of the government, represented by a prosecutor, calling a witness who is an accessory to the crime for which the defendant is charged and having that witness testify under a plea agreement – a testifying snitch.

There was a time when a U.S. Justice Department rule prohibited enforcement of the rules of professional conduct to apply to prosecutors. Imagine that, they did not have to follow known ethics. That rule was banished by Congressional enactment of the McDade Bill during October, 1998 (as the Citizen's Protection Act of 1998). Now Federal prosecutors must adhere and obey rules of professional conduct that all lawyers are required to follow. The significance of this rule is the fact that before its enactment, federal prosecutors were allowed to go to great lengths, often unethical, to prosecute and win their cases. Prosecutors for years have been free to, and did, violate professional standards that if done by defense attorneys would routinely cause defense attorneys and other attorneys to be disbarred or punished otherwise. Instead, federal prosecutors are given higher positions and higher earnings when they deprive people of their life and liberty by wrongfully taking away their civil rights and obtaining illegal convictions against them.

Of course those of us, who are currently caught in the Legal Matrix or had our run-ins, know that the damage has been done. Prosecutors have used their strength to convict many innocent people. Without a doubt, while on this mission, confidence in the Legal Matrix has been destroyed.

According to CBS NEWS.COM June 26, 2003, the following types of misconduct have been most commonly reported:

- Courtroom misconduct (making inappropriate or inflammatory comments in the presence of the jury; introducing or attempting to introduce inadmissible, inappropriate or inflammatory evidence; mischaracterizing the evidence or the facts of the case to the court or jury; committing violations pertaining to the selection of the jury; or making improper closing arguments);

- Mishandling of physical evidence (hiding, destroying or tampering with evidence, case files or court records);
- Failing to disclose exculpatory evidence;
- Threatening, badgering or tampering with witnesses;
- Using false or misleading evidence;
- Harassing, displaying bias toward, or having a vendetta against the defendant or defendant's counsel (including *selective* or *vindictive prosecution*, which includes instances of denial of a speedy trial);
- Improper behavior during grand jury proceedings.

Prosecutorial misconduct makes navigation of the Legal Matrix very difficult. In addition to the known corruption, prosecutors are allowed to use tactics that most average people would find objectionable. Take for instance the use of bribery. Although the criminal defendant's attorney is not permitted to bribe witnesses, and would be disbarred quickly if he/she did bribe a witness and was caught doing so, the same is not true for the prosecution. They are permitted and encouraged to bribe witnesses and they do this all the time.

The Informant Set Up.

A newly-arrested person (whether innocent or guilty) winds up in prison before the start of his/her criminal trial, and an informer is selected as the "lucky" cellmate. The informer, wanting to get an early release, calls up his attorney and states (falsely) that the new prisoner just confessed to him that he committed the crime for which he is charged. (It is entirely possible that the informer didn't even have a conversation with the new prisoner; all the informer has to say is that he did have a conversation with the new prisoner.) The informer also asks his attorney to pass that bit of information on to the prosecutor, and that the informer is willing to testify at the forthcoming trial in favor of the prosecution, in exchange for a reduced sentence and early release from prison for the informer.

> The prosecution then puts on this witness as the key witness against the defendant, fully realizing that the informer is lying in order to get out of prison.

As things stand now, various cases under federal law permit this bribery, but only when it is done by a federal prosecutor, and of course they don't call it bribery. If the same technique is used by defense counsel, he/she could be disbarred and sent to jail.

An amazing example of the Legal Matrix is an Ohio Court of Appeals decision, in *State of Ohio v. Berry*.[xviii] Without reference to and apparently without knowledge of 28 U.S.C. 530B[xix], the statute that upholds the bribery practice by (state) prosecutors, with the following rationale (based on 1937 and 1970 U.S. Supreme Court decisions) held:

> We have previously rejected the claim that government officials violate R.C. 2921.02(C) and DR 7-109(C) when they offer plea bargains in exchange for testimony. *State v. Drake*, 1998 Ohio App. LEXIS 6224 (Dec. 17, 1998), Franklin App. No. 98AP-448, unreported (1998 Opinions 5698, 5705).

Courts have long recognized that statutes do not apply to the government and do not affect government rights unless the text expressly includes the government. See *Nardone v. United States* (1937), 302 U.S. 379, 383, 58 S. Ct. 275, 277, 82 L. Ed. 314; Ware, at 419. This rule applies where a statute would deprive the government of a recognized or established prerogative or interest, or where applying the statute against the government would lead to an absurdity. *Nardone*, at 277.

We conclude that the use of a witness's testimony on behalf of the prosecution in exchange for a plea agreement is an established prerogative of the state. In so concluding, we recognize the rationale set forth by the United States Court of Appeals for the Sixth Circuit in *Ware*. According to the court in *Ware*, **no practice is more ingrained in our criminal justice system than the practice of the government, represented by a prosecutor, calling a witness who is an accessory to the crime for which the defendant is charged and having that witness testify under a plea agreement.** 161 F.3d at 421. The court in *Ware* also noted that the United States Supreme Court has repeatedly upheld the plea agreement practices historically utilized in our criminal justice system.

Ware, at 419, citing *Brady v. United States* (1970), 397 U.S. 742, 90 S. Ct. 1463, 25 L. Ed. 2d 747.

The courts support the use of "snitches" to testify against alleged criminals in court cases. It has been used so much that many criminal defendant's take plea offers just to head off the possibility that someone, whom they don't even know, will go into court and make untrue allegations that will support the prosecutor's charges. That is the Legal Matrix in full effect and the only way to combat this type of activity is to know the game and stay out of the way.

Overzealous Prosecutors

The estimate is that at least 10 percent of those convicted and spending long prison sentences, or waiting on death row, may be innocent. The fact of the matter is that some of the tactics used by prosecutors often lead to convictions of innocent people. Take a look at white collar crimes where the vagueness in the language of new laws make it all too easy for law enforcement officers and prosecutors to engage in misconduct which results in wrongful convictions. For instance, the U.S. Sentencing Commission's 1992 internal report determined that in 68% of the cases resulting in **"sting money laundering"** convictions, no proper representation of an unlawful activity had been made and those convicted did not know or believe that their financial transaction represented proceeds of an unlawful activity.

Author James McCloskey, director of Centurion Ministries, Inc. noted in "Convicting the Innocent" that since 1992, a plethora of additional convictions have been obtained through abusive prosecutorial practices and charges under laws such as money laundering. Often the prosecutors manipulated the high sentencing levels and even improperly charged offenses. Now with the **Patriot Act** there is a guarantee that more charges of money laundering, more investigations, interrogations and "black listing" will occur under the guise of fighting terrorism.

A study of criminal appeals from 1970 to the present revealed 441 Ohio cases in which the defendant alleged prosecutorial error or misconduct. In 71 of the cases, judges ruled a prosecutor's conduct prejudiced the defendant and these judges reversed or remanded the conviction, sentence, or indictment. In 16 of the cases, a dissenting judge or judges (not the majority opinion) thought that the prosecutor's conduct warranted reversing or remanding the defendant's conviction, sentence, or indictment. Luckily at least two of these defendants were able to prove their innocence.

The Work of One Prosecutor[xx]

Carmen Marino worked as a prosecutor in Cuyahoga County for 30 years before he retired in 2002. He served as chief prosecutor and head of the major trial division. At least 15 Ohio criminal appeals have addressed Marino's conduct. Out of those, judges reversed four defendants' convictions because of Marino's prejudicial trial arguments.

In one of Mario's cases, after a jogger found 19-year-old Tony Klann's body floating face down in a creek, the state charged three men, Ed Espinoza, Michael Keenan, and Joe D'Ambrosio, with his murder. "When you start out and you have three people involved in a crime, you're never certain who did what until somebody talks," said Marino. "Then you have to take their statement in light of the facts and see who corroborates them." Espinoza was first to talk. He said it happened while the three of them were with the victim on the bank of a creek. Espinoza said Keenan slit Klann's throat with a Bowie knife. Then as Klann was running into the water to escape, D'Ambrosio followed him to "finish him off." Espinoza said Klann screamed "Please don't kill me," as D'Ambrosio ran after him and stabbed him in the chest.

Witnesses established that before the murder, Keenan, Espinoza and D'Ambrosio were intoxicated and driving around town. Espinoza had a baseball bat and D'Ambrosio had a knife, and they were looking for a man named Paul Lewis. They said Lewis had broken into Keenan's car and stolen important papers, cocaine, and money. While driving around they came across Klann, and because Klann knew Lewis, the trio picked him up. Lewis' neighbor told police that the four men came to Lewis' residence in the middle of the night and Espinoza kicked in the door. He said D'Ambrosio was in the car holding a knife on Klann. Witnesses also established that at some point within a week of the murder, Espinoza had threatened the victim at a bar. In fact, Espinoza made such a scene that the manager kicked him out.

Marino thought that "Keenan is the real thug here," so with no eyewitness testimony and a weak case, Marino offered Espinoza a deal. If he testified against D'Ambrosio and Keenan, the state would only charge him with voluntary manslaughter. "It's an interesting situation, with respect to D'Ambrosio," Marino said. "I think he had known Keenan for only a few weeks before the incident—he's as dumb as a rock." Marino said he is careful when making deals with co-conspirators and attempts to assure that they are being truthful. "Espinoza gave his complete statement to the police before I even saw the case," Marino said.

Espinoza testified against D'Ambrosio and Keenan. In 1989, a jury convicted Keenan and sentenced him to death. "You can be pretty sure if the prosecutor is going for the death penalty, he has the facts to warrant the death penalty," Marino said. "I can't remember a capital case coming back with anything but the death penalty in any case I've tried."

After a three-day trial in 1989, a three-judge panel, including the same judge who presided over Keenan's trial, convicted D'Ambrosio and sentenced him to death. "They listen intently to the facts and take copious notes and go back and convict," Marino said. "They know we're [prosecutors] not waltzing into the courtroom on a wish and a prayer." Espinoza pleaded guilty and received a reduced sentence of 15 to 75 years. He is now out of prison.

To this day, Espinoza's account of the murder is disputed. Experts now say that Klann could not have screamed because the knife wounds caused two large holes in his trachea. Marino disagrees. "If he had been slashed below the larynx he could not scream, but the coroner testified that the slash was above the larynx, which means the sounds he made were coming out of the larynx and out of a hole in his neck," Marino said. Authorities found no forensic evidence along the creek bank where Espinoza said the murder took place and where the victim would have lost pints of blood. After searching the bank, two detectives who were first on the scene and didn't testify at the trials decided the murder could not have taken place on the creek bank.

Marino said the murder took place on the creek bank, and dismissed the lack of blood. "There are no major arteries there," Marino said, referring to Klann's neck wound. "It's not like he stood there for any length of time while he was bleeding—he was pushed into the creek."

In 1993, the Ohio Supreme Court reversed Keenan's conviction because of Marino's "gravely" prejudicial trial arguments and behavior. "I gave a pretty good closing argument," Marino said. "I took that Bowie knife and stabbed the desk with it." In the opinion that reversed Keenan's conviction, Justice Thomas Moyer wrote, "Without overwhelming evidence of guilt, we cannot know what the verdict might have been had not the prosecutor clouded the jury's vision with improper tactics." Marino said it's all just a part of the process. "This business is highly public," he said. "If you want to do something where no one is going to criticize you, be an accountant."

Keenan was later retried and re-sentenced to death. D'Ambrosio also alleged on appeal that Marino's conduct, such as improper comments and misleading assertions about Espinoza's credibility, denied him a fair trial. Courts have so far refused to address the claims because D'Ambrosio's defense attorney didn't object to Marino's statements during the trial. Both Keenan and D'Ambrosio are currently on death row.

Other Examples:

In 1982, the Ohio Supreme Court reversed Chester Liberatore's arson conviction due to Marino's "prosecutorial blunders." In the Court's opinion, Justice Clifford Brown said Marino presented a textbook example of what a closing argument should not be. However Marino said its all about interpretation. "You just get up and give a good closing argument—whoever argues best last wins." In another case, judges reversed George Kelly's conviction because Marino "purposely" offered him a chance to plead guilty to murder "in order to avoid a possible successful appeal." In May 2002, the state's Eight Circuit Appeals Court upheld Gregory Lott's murder conviction, rejecting evidence suggesting that Marino withheld exculpatory evidence from the defense, namely the victim's initial description of the attacker. In another two cases, dissenting judges would have reversed the defendants' convictions because of Marino's behavior. Marino said it's not difficult to win convictions in Ohio, as jurors are predisposed to find defendants guilty because they trust police and prosecutors. "If the person doesn't take the stand, the jury knows he is guilty," Marino said. "That's my experience."

In another case, Larry Johnson walked out of a Missouri prison during the summer of 2002, exonerated by DNA testing from a wrongful rape conviction after avowing his innocence for 18 years. St. Louis legal community insiders nodded knowingly as word trickled out who had led the prosecution back in 1984—Nels C. Moss Jr. Moss, assistant circuit attorney for the city of St. Louis and later a trial prosecutor in neighboring St. Charles County, who earned a well-deserved reputation as an aggressive, effective trial prosecutor. During his 33 years of trying cases for the people, however, he simultaneously was a recidivist breaker of the rules by which prosecutors are supposed to operate.[xxi]

After joining the St. Louis city prosecutor's office in 1968, Moss found his conduct formally challenged in at least 24 cases. In seven of those, judges reversed the conviction, declared a mistrial, or issued some other ruling adverse to the prosecution. Over the course of his career as a prosecutor, Moss reneged during trial on a pre-trial stipulation with the defense; called the jury's attention to the defendant's failure to testify, thereby compromising the Fifth Amendment rights of the accused; alluded to the defendant's uncharged criminal conduct, a violation of the rules of evidence; attacked the character of the defendant with information not in the court record; used inadmissible material from a separate trial of an accomplice; promised during jury selection or opening argument to present testimony never offered; attacked the truthfulness of defense counsel; cast aspersions on the integrity of an insanity defense; and inflamed jurors' passions during closing argument.

When one appellate panel reversed a conviction in a case won by Moss, a judge writing a concurring opinion emphasized that the blame lay with the prosecutor and not with the courts: "Most regrettable ... is the fact that we are required to remand this case for retrial, with all of the expense, delay and inconvenience attendant thereto, because of a trial incident that need not and should not have occurred ... It was a deliberate effort by one of the most experienced assistant circuit attorneys in the City of St. Louis to interject even more poison than his extensive review of defendant's prior convictions had already accomplished ... The sole purpose ... was to poison the minds of the jurors regarding the defendant's character ... Where, as in this case, the record discloses a patent effort to deprive a defendant of a fair trial, the onus for the delay and added expense should be directed toward the prosecutor who caused it. This is especially true when, rather than resulting from youthful zeal, the error is but one example of a consistent pattern of improper tactics reflected by other transcripts in cases tried by the same experienced prosecutor."

In another 17 cases prosecuted by Moss, appellate judges affirmed the conviction or trial judges allowed the proceeding to continue, despite finding Moss committed prosecutorial error.

Moss declined an interview request from the Center for Public Integrity, and wrote that he sees no point in subjecting himself to "second guessing by those that have not walked in my shoes." In his response to the interview request, Moss characterized himself as "a hard-hitting but honest prosecutor." He estimated that he tried more than 400 cases before juries, including "high-profile, racially and politically explosive cases. Obviously the friends and representatives of those convicted are dissatisfied with the outcomes and are prone to see fault and perceived injustice."

In his defense, of judges who criticized his tactics, Moss wrote that some, "have never tried cases as prosecutors or defense attorneys and have never experienced the heat of the courtroom." Moss wondered if his detractors realize that, "I have refused to proceed on numerous cases where confessions did not match the evidence, where identifications did not measure up to appropriate standards, where alibis while not conclusive have left too much reasonable doubt. ... I have never approved or sponsored testimony I suspected to be false. I have never prosecuted anyone on the basis of race; indeed most of the victims of the crimes I prosecuted were minorities."

Although Moss' record of 7 reversals due to misconduct and 17 other findings that he committed prosecutorial error is extreme, he is hardly an anomaly.

Recidivist Prosecutors

Those prosecutors who repeatedly break the rules give *recidivism*—a word usually used to describe those they work to put behind bars—a disturbing new meaning.

Local prosecutors in many of the 2,341 jurisdictions across the nation have stretched bent or broken rules while convicting defendants. Since 1970, individual judges and appellate court panels cited prosecutorial misconduct as a factor when dismissing charges at trial, reversing convictions or reducing sentences in at least 2,012 cases. The nature of the questionable conduct covers every type attributed to Moss, and more.

In 513 additional cases, appellate judges offered opinions—either dissents or concurrences—in which they found the prosecutorial misconduct serious enough to merit additional discussion; and even a reversal. In numerous other cases, judges labeled prosecutorial behavior inappropriate, but allowed the trial to continue or upheld convictions using a doctrine called, "harmless error."

The Center analyzed 11,452 cases in which charges of prosecutorial misconduct were reviewed by appellate court judges. In the majority of cases, the allegation of misconduct was ruled harmless error or was not addressed by the appellate judges, and the conviction stood. The relative rarity of reversals makes these opinions useful from an empirical standpoint. Any prosecutor who has more than one reversal to his/her credit belongs to a select club.

In 28 cases, involving 32 separate defendants, misconduct by prosecutors led to the conviction of innocent individuals who were later exonerated, the Center found. Innocent men and women were convicted of serious charges, including murder, rape, kidnapping and assault.

> 95 percent of the cases that pour in from the police never reach a jury, which means any misconduct occurs away from public view.

Guilty defendants have also had their convictions overturned. Sometimes those defendants cannot be retried because of double jeopardy rules, and are placed back on the streets of the community. In other words, prosecutorial misconduct sometimes has severe consequences for the entire community, not just a lone defendant.

In addition, the Center found some prosecutors who had convicted innocent defendants in more than one case over the course of their careers; some of these prosecutors were cited multiple times for misconduct in other cases as well.

Most of the nation's approximately 30,000 local trial prosecutors strive to balance their understandable desire to win — a desire supported by the vast majority of the citizenry — with their duty to ensure justice. There are some prosecutors, however, who have exalted winning and ignored the other half of the equation.

It is impossible to know for sure how often a specific prosecutor, (or a specific defense attorney, judge, police officer, etc.), bends or breaks the rules. In most jurisdictions, at least 95 percent of the cases that pour in from the police never reach a jury, which means any misconduct occurs away from public view. The only trial those defendants receive takes place in the prosecutor's office; the prosecutor becomes the judge and the jury. The prosecutor is the de facto law after an arrest, deciding whether to charge the suspect with committing a crime, what charge to file from a range of possibilities, whether to offer a pre-trial deal, and the terms of the deal.

Katherine Goldwasser, a law professor at Washington University in St. Louis, who served as a prosecutor in Chicago before joining academia, suggested that misconduct often occurs out of sight, especially in cases that never go to trial. Those cases by definition do not generate appellate opinions, and thus are for the most part not on the radar. "It is not a safe assumption that cases ending with guilty pleas are absent prosecutorial misconduct." [xxii]

Perhaps the most difficult type of misconduct to unearth, Goldwasser said, is the failure of the prosecutor to turn over possibly exculpatory information to the defense. Such lack of disclosure is commonly known as a "Brady violation" (After the 1963 U.S. Supreme Court case *Brady v. Maryland* and its progeny). If only police and prosecutors know about evidence that suggests innocence, how is defense counsel to know for certain such evidence even exists?

To complicate quantification, any listing of mistrials and appellate reversals involving a specific prosecutor might be incomplete. While legal databases like Lexis and Westlaw (both of which were used in this study) contain appellate rulings, some remain unpublished. Many of those that are published rarely identify the trial prosecutor. Short of visiting every courthouse in the country, there is no way to determine how many cases are dismissed or ruled mistrials by trial judges, (and thus never reaching the appellate courts), because of a prosecutor's misconduct.

Despite those limitations in the data, the study determined that, like Moss in St. Louis, other prosecutors around the country have been found by appellate court or trial court judges to have bent or broken the rules multiple times.

MORE EXAMPLES

- Appellate judges have ruled that Montgomery County, Alabama District Attorney Ellen Brooks' discriminatory tactics deprived defendants of fair trials 4 times since she began prosecuting in 1977. Former Hinds County, Mississippi, District Attorney Edward Peters was involved in 6 cases in which judges ruled that his conduct prejudiced a defendant.

- The pattern of behavior of John Zimmermann, a trial prosecutor in Davidson County (Nashville), Tennessee, so alarmed six former Tennessee prosecutors that, during July 2002, they filed an *amici curiae* brief to the U.S. Supreme Court on behalf of Death Row defendant Abu-Ali Abdur'Rahman. The six, who constitute a who's who of the Tennessee legal profession, cited Zimmermann's misconduct in the case – confirmed by the state Supreme Court but nevertheless ruled as harmless error – and his behavior in previous, unrelated cases.

The brief argued that Zimmermann withheld evidence from the defense, and misrepresented a prior conviction of the defendant. Even more troubling, it cites Zimmermann's conduct during three other, unrelated cases, including a murder case in which the verdict was overturned because of the Davidson County prosecutor's behavior. (In a response to the Center for Public Integrity, Zimmerman vociferously contests the charges.)

As the world turns and the Legal Matrix goes, in addition to dealing with the laws that affect our lives, we have to worry that the prosecutors are not so determined to get a conviction that they violate our rights, but as the above text indicates, prosecutors break laws everyday.

Prosecutors Withholding Evidence

When false testimony is not being coerced, we have to worry about the habit of prosecutors withholding evidence. The law is strict in that prosecutors must provide what is called exculpatory evidence (information that tends to prove or infer that the person charged is not guilty of the accused crime), but often they do not. Clarence Darrow was right when he said, "A courtroom is not a place where truth and innocence inevitably triumph; it is only an arena where contending lawyers fight not for justice but to win." Many times this hidden information is not only "favorable" to the defendant, but it clears him.

A case where exculpatory evidence would have helped keep an innocent man out of jail was Philadelphia's Miguel Rivera case. The district attorney withheld the fact that two shopkeepers saw the defendant outside their shop when the art museum murder was actually in progress. Another case was the Gordon Marsh case near Baltimore, Maryland.[xxiii] The state failed to tell the defendant that its main witness against him was in jail at the time she claimed she saw him running from the murder scene.

When defense attorneys are denied the ability to properly defend their clients, by having all the information and evidence, it creates another barrier to survival in the Legal Matrix.

The Use of Bail to Keep us in Jail

Prosecutors routinely seek excessive bail for the specific purpose of preventing the defendant from getting released from jail prior to trial. This makes it more difficult for the defendant to defend himself, and satisfies the purpose of tying up the defendant's assets and loan sources. This also makes it more difficult if not impossible for the defendant to hire an attorney. The purpose of bail is to ensure that a defendant appears in court for pre-trials, hearings, and trial. The amount of bail should be set with this in mind, bail should not be made so high that the defendant is unable to raise the money and be released. Prosecutors try to win their case by preventing the defendant from having the time, freedom, and resources needed to defend themselves against the prosecutors' criminal charges.[xxiv]

In some areas of the law the issue of bail has been distorted and applied in ways to ensure harm to the accused. For example, in Federal Court drug cases, there is a presumption, (before establishing any guilt or a full review of the facts of the case), that the defendant should be denied bail because, the law holds that the defendant is considered a menace to society, not necessarily a flight risk.

I must admit that there are time when a high bail is very important. Take for instance domestic violence cases. When there is a real threat to the safety of another individual the bail should be high.

In addition to police corruption and prosecutorial misconduct, the Legal Matrix itself is designed to keep us under control, accordingly, it is difficult, and once your presence is acknowledged in the Legal Matrix through a legal proceeding, to get out of the system unscathed. One reason for the unlikelihood of getting out unscathed is that there is a presumption of guilt. Regardless of the fact that the constitution has safeguards for fair trials, and that everyone is constitutionally presumed innocent, once accusations are made and the person is actually brought to trial, the natural tendency of people and prospective juries is to believe that the person must be guilty of something, or else there would be no charges. That's why so many defendants can not make bail. In some cases it is justified, in others it is excessive.

Witnesses who Lie

It should be obvious that prosecutor's witnesses, other than police officers, also give false testimony in exchange for immunity or reduced sentences. Common criminals, who are in deep trouble themselves, with the same prosecutor's office or local police authority, are often employed as star state witnesses. In exchange for their false testimony, their own charges are dismissed. They are also given non-custodial or greatly reduced prison sentences. An even more surprising fact is that even non-criminals give false testimony.

I introduced you to Clarence Bradley earlier, when we discussed the bad police report, but here is the rest of the story. In 1981, while investigating a murder of a student, three white high school janitors were threatened by the Texas Rangers into testifying that they saw Clarence Bradley, their black custodial supervisor, walking into the restroom, the area of the high school where the victim had entered only minutes before she disappeared. Bradley was convicted and sentenced to death based on the inferential testimony that, since he was the last person seen near the victim, he must have killed her. Eight years later Bradley was exonerated by the judge who conducted his evidentiary hearing when one of these janitors came forward, and told how they had lied in implicating Bradley because of coercion by the investigating law officer.

In northwestern Louisiana, a white rural town, a man named Wing had his guilt determined based on the testimony of his wife. After Wing was convicted, his common-law wife came forward on the eve of his execution, and admitted that she had lied at his trial five years earlier. She stated she lied because the deputy sheriff threatened to put her in jail, and forever separate her from her children unless she regurgitated at trial what he wanted her to say.

In the Terry McCracken case, in the suburbs of Philadelphia, a fellow high school student of McCracken testified that he saw McCracken flee the convenience store moments after a customer was shot to death during the course of a robbery. The teenager was induced to manufacture this false eyewitness account after three visits to the police station. Among the evidence that vindicated McCracken was the confessions by the real robbers/killers.

So, you see, it not only can happen anywhere, it happens everywhere. It is not only the recognizable agents, prosecutors, police, and judges who are determined to put you away. There are times when everyday citizens become Agents of the systems and work for the benefit of the Legal Matrix by lying, and giving false statements. (Be careful who your friends are).

Answer - The Agents Can't Be Trusted

The question is can Agents be trusted? A colleague of mine believes the negative of this question. He believes that once you are involved in the Legal Matrix as an Agent, you lose your scene of struggle and dedication to the overall good of everyone and instead, become infatuated with the new power. That's what happens to all of us, African American, White, you name it. The Legal Matrix intoxicates us and makes us act with forgetfulness. We forget we are servants, forget we were not always in a position of power and forget the Legal Matrix can reach up and grab you at any place and any time.

There is hope. In the City of Cleveland a friend and colleague Anthony Jordan, a Morehouse and Howard Law educated attorney, was appointed to the position of Chief Prosecutor for the City of Cleveland, Ohio. When questioned about his new position, he eloquently stated, "I will use this opportunity to seek justice, not merely to seek convictions." The opportunity came when R & B sensation Gerald Levert was charged with drunken driving, impeding traffic, obstructing police business and resisting arrest. He also faced a felonious-assault charge accusing him of punching an officer in the face. City Prosecutor Anthony Jordan refused to bring the felonious assault charges. He said there was no evidence the singer caused serious physical harm to the officers.

The County did pick up the case, but that is another story.

Chapter III
The Laws of the Legal Matrix
The Design of the Legal Matrix
The Desert of the Real

In *The Matrix* movie, the desert of the real was a glimpse into the behind the scenes true reality of the world. For our purposes, the desert of the real forces us to see life as it truly is. This book brings you the desert of the real, a look at the essence of the life in which we live. Remember, most of us travel through life unaware of the Legal Matrix – the system designed to control us. Many are not aware of the fact that at any given time the system can utilize its tools to control our lives.

> "The system will push and push and instigate until they are able to utilize the tool necessary to gain control."

The Attack Against Hip Hop - part I

An example of the desert of the real is a statement by the Minister Louis Farrakhan in a recent Black Entertainment Television (BET) interview. The subject of the interview was the hip hop feud between two talented, and influential artists 50 cent and Ja Rule. Similar to the beef between Biggie and Tupac, this war based on media hype, escalated into real violence. The Minister was conducting an interview with Ja Rule and in an attempt to ease the tension between the two rappers he made a profound statement. The Minister described the situation between the two rappers by stating that, "the system will push, and push, and instigate until they are able to utilize the tool necessary to gain control." In other words, this beef between the two rappers who are young, rich and influential will be pushed to the point where the Legal Matrix will step in and use the laws that exist to crush them both.

The Legal Matrix

Minister Farrakhan believes that there is an attack on the hip hop community, just as there was an attack on the Nation of Islam. The truth is that the Legal Matrix does not take kindly to individuals who are living outside the law. To establish control, the Legal Matrix will destroy tax havens, cut down on allowances and do anything and everything imaginable to bring you in. In addition to the musicians we hear about, some athletes are living outside the law. Look at Allen Iverson, a successful athlete who has continuously expressed his dismay with the system, and who has not been afraid to voice his opinion. The result was criminal charges and allegations brought against him, a public outcry against his music CD, and the fact that Madison Avenue has not embraced him like the advertising world has embraced other athletes. Even politically astute comedian Chris Rock mentioned in one of his standup concerts that this government will take perfectly legal activities, and push it to the center, and make it illegal in order to maintain control.

What is the desert of the real? What is the real deal in the Legal Matrix? For starters, look at the fact that an estimated 6.6 million Americans live under the control of the current criminal justice system either in jail, in prison or on parole or probation. The majority of this population is going back and forth between courts, prisons, and parole. That is the real.

Parole and probation are not just simple functions of prison. Instead, each is a component in the system. They amplify and eat each other as criminal law has become more punitive and surveillance and policing have grown. When you are convicted of a felony, you have fewer opportunities when you return to the community. On top of that, for some felonies in Ohio, your driver's license will be suspended and you will be on post release supervision when you get out of jail. What is the problem with that scenario? The Legal Matrix will keep feeding itself. If you come out of jail under the same oppressive conditions as you were under in jail, with the only difference being that you have more opportunity to get in trouble, how free are you? That is the desert of the real, that is the brutal reality of the Legal Matrix.

The number of people incarcerated for violating parole or other release conditions is on the rise. Consider the system in California to control the waves of "out of jail" members of the community. California is divided into four parole regions policed by 2000 armed parole and Agents. The bottom line is that increased surveillance and computer databases are causing armed force units to target selected individuals in the community and making them subject to prosecution.

The success of hip hop and its emergence into the suburbs of America make the artists more threatening. It is a vicious cycle. The artists know that being a threat sells records, so they create more dramatic and shocking lyrics. Nevertheless, the fact remains that some and many artists are targets of the Legal Matrix. They are watched at parties, followed, investigated and monitored. When a person chooses this industry as a career, he/she is opening himself up to great scrutiny.

Building the Legal Matrix Through the Courts

The advance of the Legal Matrix came to my attention in the eighties when the conservative judges of the Supreme Court handed down decisions that strengthened the ability to prosecute alleged criminals. The decision in *Gates v. Illinois*[xxv] made it easier for police to obtain search warrants based on anonymous tips. How could we ensure that the tips are accurate, or more importantly not the imagination of the police? Obviously we can not ever be sure and, therefore, police will continue to exploit this reality.

In *United States v. Leon*[xxvi] the police were allowed to use a defective warrant to obtain evidence. The problem with that decision is easy to identify, if the facts are wrong, or there is a mistake, there can be no true probable cause that the person actually did what they were accused of. However, based on this decision, police now have an exception to the rule that allows the suppression of evidence that was illegally obtained by being allowed to go forward with mistakes and incorrect facts. This is the system correcting itself so to achieve its primary goal - control.

In 1984, the Comprehensive Crime Control Act made some of the most sweeping, and dramatic changes to the criminal justice system that had lasting effects. Among its provisions, the bill created federal protective detention (criminals considered a risk to the community would be denied bail), established mandatory minimums (which keep the judiciary from sentencing convicted persons based on individual considerations), eliminated federal parole, increased mandatory minimums for drug offenses, and beefed up the charges for drugs (increasing the penalties for crack cocaine versus the penalty for powder). The affect of these laws still resonate today. For instance, if you are charged with a drug related offense, the judge may use this law to refuse bail to an otherwise deserving person, someone who many have never been convicted of a crime before.

In 1986, the Anti-Drug Abuse Act imposed 29 new mandatory minimums sentences. Among them a 5-year mandatory minimum for offenses involving 100 grams of heroin, 500 grams of cocaine or 5 grams of crack. Additionally, for federal drug crimes involving physical injuries or death, or for major second offenses that mandatory minimum was increased to 20 years. It is no secret that in 1980, when these laws were passed, African Americans accounted for about 12% of the population and over 23% of all those arrested on drug charges. In 1990, African Americans were still about 12% of the population, but accounted for 40% of the drugs busts and 60% of the convictions.

When I was younger and living in East Cleveland, Ohio there was a saying among drug dealers that certain nights were called "vice night." This term meant that during certain times of the year, certain days of the weeks, and hours of the night, police forces would beef up the activity against suspected drug dealers. This activity is not unique to East Cleveland. In Los Angeles, New York and "ghettos" across the country, law enforcement teams would conduct heavy raids arresting numerous small drug dealers and drug users in an attempt to stop the drug problem in America. In these cities, the arrest numbers reached the thousands in a matter of months and every night became vice night.

> I'm one of those negros that's allowed into certain places, but if I start believing the hype, like I'm the 'special negro,' then I could end up just like that."
> - P. Diddy

Adding to these laws was the strengthening of forfeiture laws that helped many states seize millions of dollars in assets, often when there was no connection with the drug business.

The design of the Legal Matrix in and of itself presents problems that could easily cause outrage to U.S. citizens, so the Agents must drum up support for controversial laws, and actions that they utilize. The usefulness of and the strength of the Legal Matrix was demonstrated in dramatic fashion during President George Bush's (the first one) first major speech. The Bush team had the DEA set up a drug bust in Lafayette Park, across the street from the White House. The victim of the set up was a 17 year old high school student named Keith Johnson. The set up was reported by Michael Isikoff, in the September 22, 1989 of the *Washington Post*. It was called a set up because it became knowledge that the young man was never inclined to sell drugs in that area, at that particular time, but he was entrapped into the situation in order to spear the media hype. It was done to give the Legal Matrix the ammunition and spin control to continue to create and strengthen the laws that affect us.

Even today we see spin control by the government on issues such as the abuse of Iraqi prisoners, justification of the Iraq war, and support of the Patriot Act. In fact, to date at least 108 people have died in American custody in Iraq and Afghanistan, most of them violently, according to government data provided to The Associated Press March 16, 2005. In addition to the spin control used to temper the American public, the Legal Matrix gets funding in the millions of dollars in budgetary support each year to keep you in control. The DEA, FBI, US Marshals, Customs, and Federal Prosecutors are all fully funded and fully operational. For example, in 1990 the total federal anti-narcotic spending was totaled at $8.8 billion. Drug busts across the nation increased dramatically as evidenced by the fact that, in 1990, California's prison system added 300 new inmates per week.

The Legal Matrix's design is really simple: laws, rules and regulations are in place. They dictate our total existence. It is not designed to give us absolute freedom. We can work with in the design to achieve success, peace, and freedom. Don't underestimate the Legal Matrix – the design will take away your life and liberty in a heart beat. It was eloquently put by P. Diddy, in the July 2004 issue of Vibe Magazine. P. Diddy was asked why he had a picture of O.J. Simpson among the inspirational pictures on his dressing room wall (the dressing room he occupied at the Royale Theater during his staring role in *A Raisin in the Sun*), he replied that "it's a constant reminder of what they can do to you if you ever get too comfortable. I'm one of those negros that's allowed into certain places, but if I start believing the hype, like I'm the 'special negro,' then I could end up just like that."

As a result of the design of the Legal Matrix, the population in federal prisons has quadrupled from 43,000 inmates in 1987, to over 173,000 today - at a cost to taxpayers of $4 billion a year. How did that happen? In the wake of the cocaine epidemic of the 1980s, Congress passed harsh sentencing guidelines and mandatory-minimum sentencing laws - requiring federal judges in most cases to impose long jail terms on anyone convicted of drug trafficking, no matter how small their crime. Judge Patrick Murphy, the chief judge of the federal district court in East St. Louis, Illinois, doles out long sentences nearly every week to drug dealers and traffickers. He says those sentences haven't helped in his district: "You're in East St. Louis. East St. Louis is crime-ridden, poverty-stricken, violent, dirty, dangerous, and here the sentences are the longest and the hardest anywhere in the federal judiciary … Here, prosecutions happen regularly. Sentences are meted out long and hard. Hardest sentences in the United States, right here."[xxvii]

The interesting part about the argument in support of the tough drug sentences and laws is that the laws are not taking the real drug dealers out of the game. "What passes for a drug king in 99 percent of the cases is nothing more than a young man who can't even afford a lawyer when he's hauled into court. I've seen very few drug kings," says Judge Murphy. What he does see, however, is defendant after defendant like Brenda Valencia, who served 11 years of a 12 year - 7 month sentence for giving a drug dealer a ride - twice as many years as she would have gotten if she'd killed someone and been convicted of manslaughter.

> **"What passes for a drug king in 99 percent of the cases is nothing more than a young man who can't even afford a lawyer when he's hauled into court. I've seen very few drug kings."** Judge Patrick Murphy.

The Programs

Programs are the ways by which the Legal Matrix controls us. They are, so to speak, the meat of the Legal Matrix. The Legal Matrix would not exist without the programs that enforce its purpose of control. We talked about the Agents and the design; well the programs are part of the design. If we attempt to discuss all the programs, from traffic laws to tax regulations, this text would be quite lengthy therefore; we will discuss some of the programs that most affect our existence in the Legal Matrix.

The Good Programs

Legal Matrix has no heart or emotions, it just is. It is just the system that is in place to control our lives, and to ensure that there is no or, at least, minimal chaos. Because the Legal Matrix has no heart, there are some parts of the system that actually help us accomplish certain things or

> Most people were never told in driver's education class that breaking traffic laws can result in jail time. Most of the programs in the Legal Matrix can lead to incarceration or loss of liberty.

our goals – these are the programs that work for our benefit. In the movie *The Matrix*, the oracle speaks about programs that do what they are supposed to do. They function without flaw or evidence of the control system. Basically, these programs work without our knowledge of it. For example, traffic control devises do what they are supposed to do, and a large part of this program is for our benefit. Whether they are stop signs, stop lights, yield signs, or speed limits that jump from 45 to 25 in a matter of feet. They are programs designed to do what they do - regulate the traffic.

Beneath the surface, further inside the program, the actual language or affect is that if you break these simple traffic laws you will suffer a cost. You may be fined monetarily, lose your license to drive, or end up in jail. Is the purpose of the program just to provide safety (working for our benefit), or to control or punish us? The answer is very simple. The programs in the Legal Matrix serve dual purposes. Remember the Legal Matrix is all around us, and there are needs that will be served by the Legal Matrix and debts to be paid because of it. On the surface, we don't see the inner workings of these programs until certain other events happen and shed light on the true purpose of the programs and the underlying system that controls it. For instance, we do not appreciate the yield signs that slow our mobility and progress, yet we are grateful for that program when it prevents an accident.

One of the purposes of this text is to provide information, and exposure to the risks of the Legal Matrix. The programs that exist are for the purpose of control and the moment we travel outside the guidelines of the programs, we are exposed to penalties. Most people were never told in driver's education class that breaking traffic laws can result in jail time. In fact, most of the programs in the Legal Matrix, (other laws), like traffic violations, can lead to incarceration or loss of liberty if we are not mindful of the potential to get caught in the Legal Matrix.

The Other Programs

The War on Drugs

Cocaine seized by the Drug Enforcement Agency
Photo: DEA.gov

"You were caught with the drugs, you are a drug dealer, and it is illegal to deal drugs, period."

The system is working fast and hard to maintain a level of control over all of us. The war on drugs is real, and the program is fully functional. That fact is particularly real in the situation with people dealing in drugs. We all know that drugs are illegal, the use of drugs destroy lives, and the ripple effect of this industry is destroying neighborhoods in our community. To put it point blank – illegal drugs are wrong. To combat this wrong the Legal Matrix is in full swing to control this problem. The answer has been to create and promote strict drug laws and penalties.

The penalties in the Federal system are very severe. Across the country, on the state level, the laws are just as strong. I am contacted by clients on a weekly basis concerning drug cases that include mandatory time for both state and federal cases. My first response has to be the obvious, and I believe that most attorneys think the same way, "you were caught with the drugs, you are a drug dealer, and it is illegal to deal drugs, period."

I am an attorney who believes strongly in our individual rights, otherwise I wouldn't have written this book. I fight long and hard to ensure that, in a particular drug case, the police officers did not violate my client's rights while bringing the case against him. I will fight to the end. However, the chips are sometimes stacked against you.

Regardless of what any attorney tells a client, all things being equal, the only way to get a case thrown out when drugs are found is to show that something illegal was done when and by the way the officer found the drugs. Second and most important, the ability to get the case thrown out depends on the judge who hears the evidence. Suppression is not an issue for a jury of peers. Suppression of evidence is heard by a judge, and if the judge does not agree that your rights were violated the evidence will remain against you. If the evidence remains you will be forced to go to trial, plead, or fight from jail by way of appeal.

Many young men and women in our society have several misunderstandings in regard to drug laws and cases. The following are some of the most common myths.

MYTH 1:   DEA and other Agents have to tell you that they are working under cover.

MYTH 2:   You have a right to bond release on federal drug charges.

MYTH 3:   If you are not caught with drugs there is no case against you. Remember possession and constructive possession.

MYTH 4:   Crime pays.

MYTH 5:   The system is fair – it is not, take a look at the chart below.

The American Civil Liberties Union has argued that lowering powder minimums under the current racially uneven enforcement patterns would have the effect of increasing the number of minorities in prison. [21] Indeed, as the Commission's 2000 report shows, even though the black proportion (30.3%) of powder cases is much lower than that for crack, most of the white defendants are ethnically Hispanic (50.6%) - which means the total minority proportion of powder cases is 81% (see Figure 4).[22] Assuming law enforcement practices in the drug market remained the same, it would be the case that instead of decreasing disparities for African American and Hispanic communities, decreasing the amount of powder required to trigger minimum sentences would actually increase disparities.

Figure 4
Race/Ethnicity of Cocaine Offenders
Fiscal Year 2000

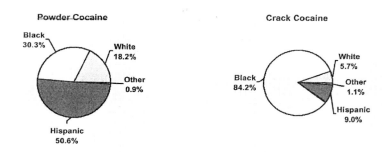

SOURCE: U.S. Sentencing Commission 2000 Sourcebook of Federal Sentencing Statistics.

---

[20] Testimony of Kathy Hawk Sawyer before the Subcommittee on the Departments of Commerce, Justice, and State, The Judiciary and Related Agencies of the Committee on Appropriations. Washington, D.C.: U.S. Government Printing Office: 2000.

[21] American Civil Liberties Union, Press Release, March 19, 2002.

[22] U.S. Sentencing Commission 2000 Sourcebook of Federal Sentencing Statistics.

This graph speaks to the inconsistency in which drug laws are enforced in this country. The truth of the matter is that the laws and the way they are applied are not fair. If we dispel the myths that are listed, and become knowledgeable about the truth of drug laws and cases, you will have to make an informed decision before entering this industry. I believe your choice will be to stay clear of the illegal drugs and the war on drugs program of the Legal Matrix.

The Misplaced War and Origins of Cocaine

Whether it was by negligence or chance, the fact remains that cocaine and made its way into the United States by some outside force, it was not manufactured here, it is not grown here. There is the theory that the U.S. government was, partially, involved in the introduction of this drug to Los Angeles, California, or possibly responsible for the drugs entry into this country based on the government's willful negligence.

The theory goes as follows: In the 1980's the new drug, crack cocaine, appeared on the streets at a time when many youth in the inner city were being forced into the underground economy to survive. An investigation reporter, Gary Webb of the San Jose Mercury News revealed that Nicaraguan agents working with the United States Central Intelligence Agency (CIA) sold tons of cocaine in the United States during the 80's and shipped the profits to the CIA Nicaraguan Contras. Webb's work was based on "declassified reports, federal court testimony, undercover tapes, court records here and abroad, and hundreds of hours of interviews." His report presented the following assertions

- He uncovered the names of Contra operatives who bought tons of cocaine from Columbian drug lords and passed it on to various drug-dealing networks within the United States,
- Cocaine was flown into Texas airfields,
- Contra dealers, at various times, met with CIA agents,

- Tons of cheap cocaine flowed like a river into ghettos in Los Angeles and beyond,
- Testimony from Oscar Danilo Blandon, the Contra operative directly in charge of selling cocaine in Los Angeles, revealed that the drug ring sold almost a ton of cocaine in the United States at a value of $54 million,
- Known dealers from Nicaragua were allowed visas to enter the United States,
- Cornel Oliver North had memos that suggest knowledge of drugs being smuggled into the United States by planes.

More information is available in an article called, *"Dark Alliance"* that appeared in the San Jose Mercury News, August 18-20.

For what it's worth, this information reveals that many police forces in the United States tried to stop the drug trafficking, but for reasons unknown to this author, and others, the effort to thwart drug sales and entry were not successful. Additionally there were a few prosecutions at the top level who tried to deal with the situation. In fact, to this day there are still very few prosecutions at the top levels of drug distribution fighting the batter; most of the battles are waged against the low level dealers in our communities.

So it should be of no surprise that at the climax of this newly introduced drug activity, the government launched its war on drugs by sending forces into the communities, setting extreme legal penalties for the sale of crack and ultimately locking up thousands of young men and women, mostly African American, in federal and state prisons.

As I said many police forces in the United States tried to stop the cocaine entrance into this country and even the high level trafficking. However, they were fighting a losing battle. At the climax of this activity, the government launched its war on drugs by sending forces into the communities, setting extreme legal penalties of crack and ultimately locking up thousands of young men and women, mostly black, in federal and state prisons.

Whether you believe the cocaine conspiracy pundits or not, the truth is that this drug had its introduction into this country by unusual means, and African Americans are being imprisoned and paying for the existence of this drug more than any other race of people.

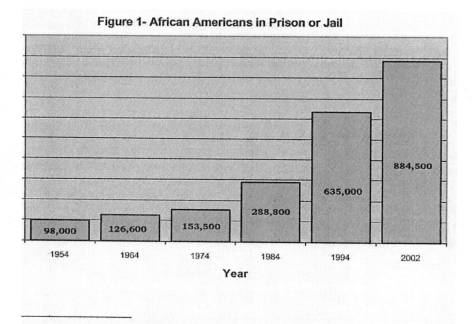

Figure 1- African Americans in Prison or Jail

odology section for a description of the population estimates.

It costs nearly $9 billion per year to keep drug law violators behind bars, yet 55% of all federal drug defendants are classified as low-level offenders, such as mules or street dealers. Only 11% are classified as high-level dealers.[xxviii] These statistics prove that the war on drugs is being fought against the wrong people and groups.

There is no way the sale or use of drugs in this country will be controlled in any realistic and measurable manner by targeting the low-level drug dealers in the ghetto. The only way to put a dent in this business is to stop the drugs at the border.

The Program called Conspiracy Laws

In 1988, Congress passed another pre-election Anti-Drug Law. One of the provisions was urged by the Department of Justice to simply close a little loophole. The change was to apply the mandatory sentences of 1986, intended for high level traffickers, to include anyone who was a member of a drug trafficking conspiracy. The effect of this amendment was to make everyone in a conspiracy liable for every act of the conspiracy. For example, if a defendant is simply the doorman at a crack house, he is liable for the entire amount of crack ever sold from that crack house, and he is liable for the entire amount of crack ever sold by the organization that runs the crack house. After the conspiracy amendment was enacted the prison population swelled. Within 6 years, the number of drug cases in federal prisons increased by 300%. From 1986 to 1998 it was up by 450%.

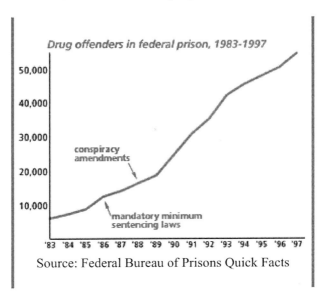

Source: Federal Bureau of Prisons Quick Facts

One result of the conspiracy amendment is that low-level traffickers can get very long sentences. They can also be the victims of lies by codefendants who have figured out how to cut a deal, and manipulate the sentencing laws to their advantage. With the conspiracy laws in effect, high-level traffickers often get lower sentences than Congress anticipated. The top organizer is in a position, for example, to identify and testify against the people who launder money for him at a bank, corrupt police officers, airport or shipping personnel, and others. When a top organizer faces a very long mandatory sentence, he is able to offer "substantial assistance," and in turn get a low sentence. One example of such deals were the much reduced sentences of high level cocaine traffickers who testified against former Panamanian strongman, General Manuel Noriega, when the U.S. government prosecuted him for cocaine trafficking.

So with the conspiracy laws, our life in the Legal Matrix can be jeopardized if, on the lower end, we simply make the wrong phone call or have the wrong conversation. On the higher end, if we are involved with people who are conducting illegal drug activity we are risking our freedom.

What are the Sentencing Guidelines, and how do they relate to mandatory minimum sentences?

A 2003 report by Human Rights Watch found that the United States has the highest rate of incarceration in the world. More than half of all federal inmates are there from conviction of drug crimes. Of that number, 58% have no history of violence or high-level drug dealing. This is the Legal Matrix at work.

Our commander in-chief, President George W. Bush favors the status-quo mandatory minimums as a way to control drug crimes and "punish those who deal in death." Critics of mandatory minimums cite a system where the hands of judges are effectively tied, and parole is not an option. As it stands now, judges defer their sentencing authority to Congress' across-the-board formula, which means they aren't able to make special considerations regarding an individual defendant's case.

Plainly put, the penalties in the Legal Matrix are stiff and largely unfair. In a 2002 report to Congress, the U.S. Sentencing Commission, an independent agency within the federal government, found the current trigger ratio between cocaine and crack cocaine to be inappropriate and recommended revising the levels. The commission found that in the year 2000, three-quarters of federal crack cocaine offenders had no link to weapons. The biggest link seems to be between crack and race: 85 percent of crack offenders in 2000 were black. The commission warned that the current penalty scheme caused a perception of racial disparity that might foster distrust in the criminal system.

It is imperative that the grandfather of all programs, the sentencing laws, is discussed in relation to the Legal Matrix. The ability to sentence is the ability to take away our liberty, our freedom. The imposition of a prison sentence is the most severe of the programs in the Legal Matrix. This program is taking its toll on our citizens.

In the 60s, 70s, and 80s, many people, who looked at the justice system, were concerned in the way that different federal judges gave very different sentences to people who committed very similar crimes. This might be because the judges were in different parts of the country, or because they had very different theories about just punishment. In some cases, the differences may have been a result of racial prejudice.

After many years of debate, Congress, in 1984, formed a commission to create a system of sentencing that would be applied the same way by federal judges around the country. Crimes would be analyzed, depending upon specified criteria. For example, if the defendant carried a gun during a crime, but didn't fire it at anyone a guideline for an appropriate sentence would be created. Judges would have to determine the facts of the case, the facts about the offender including the offender's history of prior offenses, and find the appropriate guideline range which would set forth a narrow range of months from which a sentence may be imposed. If a judge finds a reason to depart from the guideline, he or she may do so, but the reason must be put on the record. Sentences that depart from the guidelines can be appealed.

In drug cases, sentencing guidelines are tied to the quantity of drugs involved in an offense. In a series of steps, the more drugs involved, the longer the sentence. For the principal drugs of abuse -- heroin, marijuana, cocaine, LSD, methamphetamine, PCP -- the quantity steps of the guidelines build upon the various quantity triggers of the mandatory minimum sentences. For example, 100 kilograms of marijuana in a drug offense triggers a mandatory minimum sentence of 5 years, and 1000 pounds of marijuana trigger a mandatory sentence of 10 years. Therefore, smuggling 700 pounds of marijuana triggers a guideline sentence of between 78 and 97 months but a mandatory minimum sentence of 5 years. The judge could depart below the 78 months, but could not go below 5 years. Only if the prosecution says the defendant offered "substantial assistance" in the prosecution of another offender could the judge sentence the defendant to less than 5 years.

SENTENCING TABLE
(in months of imprisonment)

Offense Level	Criminal History Category (Criminal History Points)					
	I (0 or 1)	II (2 or 3)	III (4, 5, 6)	IV (7, 8, 9)	V (10, 11, 12)	VI (13 or more)
1	0-6	0-6	0-6	0-6	0-6	0-6
2	0-6	0-6	0-6	0-6	0-6	1-7
3	0-6	0-6	0-6	0-6	2-8	3-9
4	0-6	0-6	0-6	2-8	4-10	6-12
5	0-6	0-6	1-7	4-10	6-12	9-15
6	0-6	1-7	2-8	6-12	9-15	12-18
7	0-6	2-8	4-10	8-14	12-18	15-21
8	0-6	4-10	6-12	10-16	15-21	18-24
9	4-10	6-12	8-14	12-18	18-24	21-27
10	6-12	8-14	10-16	15-21	21-27	24-30
11	8-14	10-16	12-18	18-24	24-30	27-33
12	10-16	13-18	15-21	21-27	27-33	30-37
13	12-18	15-21	18-24	24-30	30-37	33-41
14	15-21	18-24	21-27	27-33	33-41	37-46
15	18-24	21-27	24-30	30-37	37-46	41-51
16	21-27	24-30	27-33	33-41	41-51	46-57
17	24-30	27-33	30-37	37-46	46-57	51-63
18	27-33	30-37	33-41	41-51	51-63	57-71
19	30-37	33-41	37-46	46-57	57-71	63-78
20	33-41	37-46	41-51	51-63	63-78	70-87
21	37-46	41-51	46-57	57-71	70-87	77-96
22	41-51	46-57	51-63	63-78	77-96	84-105
23	46-57	51-63	57-71	70-87	84-105	92-115
24	51-63	57-71	63-78	77-96	92-115	100-125
25	57-71	63-78	70-87	84-105	100-125	110-137
26	63-78	70-87	78-97	92-115	110-137	120-150
27	70-87	78-97	87-108	100-125	120-150	130-162
28	78-97	87-108	97-121	110-137	130-162	140-175
29	87-108	97-121	108-135	121-151	140-175	151-188
30	97-121	108-135	121-151	135-168	151-188	168-210
31	108-135	121-151	135-168	151-188	168-210	188-235
32	121-151	135-168	151-188	168-210	188-235	210-262
33	135-168	151-188	168-210	188-235	210-262	235-293
34	151-188	168-210	188-235	210-262	235-293	262-327
35	168-210	188-235	210-262	235-293	262-327	292-365
36	188-235	210-262	235-293	262-327	292-365	324-405
37	210-262	235-293	262-327	292-365	324-405	360-life
38	235-293	262-327	292-365	324-405	360-life	360-life
39	262-327	292-365	324-405	360-life	360-life	360-life
40	292-365	324-405	360-life	360-life	360-life	360-life
41	324-405	360-life	360-life	360-life	360-life	360-life
42	360-life	360-life	360-life	360-life	360-life	360-life
43	life	life	life	life	life	life

Zones (left margin): Zone A, Zone B, Zone C, Zone D

The above sentencing chart describes the unforgiving system of federal sentencing. The chart dictates how long of a prison sentence a person will receive for various crimes. The column titled "offense level" represents a congressional value for the type of offense that was committed. The criminal history category" is a calculation of the person's exposure to jail time based on that person's past criminal history.

Offense Level

Every event considered a crime to the federal government has a category for sentencing purposes. From threatening to tamper with the public water system (Offense level 10) to first degree murder (Offense level 43), the government has ranked and rated every crime imaginable. The offense levels that interest most people are those involving violation of drug laws. From a level 6 for small quantities of marijuana to level 38 for amounts of heroin or cocaine, the drug penalties have some of the most far reaching and devastating penalties in this system.

Criminal History Category

A person's criminal history category is a culmination of that person's history of legal mistakes and mishaps. From misdemeanors that result in over thirty days of incarceration to any and every conviction and sentence, every mistake you have made will count against you. While practicing law, I have come across people who have argued that it should be considered double jeopardy to culminate all past criminal offenses, but this ranking is not a new trial of your prior offense but instead just a risk analysis.

The Birth of Mandatory Minimum Sentences

The worst aspect of the sentencing laws would be the mandatory minimum sentences. These mandatory minimum sentences came about in 1986, when the Democrats in Congress saw a political opportunity to outflank Republicans by "getting tough on drugs" after basketball star Len Bias died of a cocaine overdose. It was this event that spear headed the campaign of fear prompting an out cry for tougher drug laws.

In the 1984 election, the Republicans had successfully accused Democrats of being soft on crime. The most important

Democratic political leader, House Speaker "Tip" O'Neill, was from Boston, Massachusetts. The Boston Celtics had signed Bias. During the July congressional recess, O'Neill's constituents were so consumed with anger and dismay about Bias' death, O'Neill realized how powerful an anti-drug campaign would be.

O'Neill knew that for Democrats to take credit for an anti-drug program in November elections, the bill had to get out of both Houses of Congress by early October. That required action on the House floor by early September, which meant that committees had to finish their work before the August recess. Since the idea was born in early July, the law-writing committees had less than a month to develop the ideas, to write the bills to carry out those ideas, and to get comments from the relevant government agencies and the public at large.

One idea was considered for the first time by the House Judiciary Committee four days before the recess began, it had tremendous political appeal as "tough on drugs." This was the creation of mandatory minimum sentences in drug cases. It was a type of penalty that had been removed from federal law in 1970 after extensive and careful consideration. But in 1986, no hearings were held on this idea. No experts on the relevant issues, no judges, no one from the Bureau of Prisons, or from any other office in the government provided advice on the idea before it was rushed through the committee and into law. Only a few comments were received on an informal basis. After bouncing back and forth between the Democratic controlled House and the Republican controlled Senate as each party jockeyed for political advantage. The Anti- Drug Abuse Act of 1986 finally passed both houses a few weeks before the November elections.

A mandatory minimum sentence is a minimum number of years, typically 5 or 10 years in prison that must be served when a person is convicted of a particular crime. Mandatory minimum sentences for drug crimes are based on the amount of drugs involved. Different drugs have different set quantities that trigger a specific minimum sentence. Here is a summary of some drug violation mandatory minimums.

	Type of Drug	5-year Sentence	10 year sentence
	MARIJUANA	100 plants/kilos	1000 plants or 1000 kilos
	CRACK	5 grams	50 grams
	POWER COCAINE	500 grams	5 kilos
	HEROIN	100 grams	1 kilo
	LSD	1 grams	10 grams
	METH	10 grams	100 grams
	PCP	10 grams	100 grams

The idea behind mandatory minimum sentences was to encourage the government to prosecute high level drug offenders. However, as the chart reveals, the high-level drug offenders (those who ship in the pure drugs), receive "softer" penalties than the young men pushing the drugs on the streets. For example, a drug offender could receive 5 years in federal prison for selling as little as 5 grams of crack cocaine. 5 grams might be only 25 doses of crack, depending on purity, worth a few hundred dollars. This is not what high level traffickers are involved in. Most drug cases involve low level offenders. In a report issued in 1995, the U.S. Sentencing Commission found that only 11% of federal drug trafficking defendants were major traffickers. More than half were low-level offenders.

The mandatory minimum sentences were criticized by the U.S. Sentencing Commission as early as 1991. In this report the commission found that all defense lawyers, and nearly half of prosecutors queried had serious problems with mandatory minimum sentences. Most of the judges pronounced them "manifestly unjust." The 1991 sentencing report particularly criticized the transfer of power in courts from judges - who are supposed to be impartial - to prosecutors, who are not. In response to some of the criticism in 1994 Congress enacted a "safety-valve" provision permitting relief from mandatory minimums for certain non-violent, first-time drug offenders. Democratic Representative Maxine Waters of California is one lawmaker speaking out against mandatory minimums. She recently introduced legislation to repeal mandatory minimums in favor of restoring discretion to individual judges. Waters had introduced a similar bill before, but it was never voted on.

Judge John Martin, a republican appointee who resigned from the bench in light of the new law by congress that makes it harder for federal judges to impose lighter sentences, stated "Judges throughout the country, of all political persuasions, feel that they have to have discretion so that they can do justice in the individual cases." It is unjust. It's taking people who are low-level violators and putting them in jail for 15-20 years. I had a situation where a defendant was an addict. He sat on his stoop. People came to him and said "do you know where I can buy some crack?' He told them about an apartment where there was crack being sold. For this, the people who sold it every once in a while gave him some crack for his own personal use. The guideline range for that man was 16 years, that doesn't seem to me like justice."

Our sentences in this country are too long and the laws are not reducing the sale of drugs in this country. In 1986, lead attorney for the House Subcommittee on Narcotics, Eric Sterling helped write the mandatory-minimum drug legislation. He has left Congress, and is now working to change the laws. He called it "the worst legislation I've ever been involved with and it's probably the worst thing I've ever done professional as a lawyer."[xxix] Last August one of the U.S. Supreme Court Judges, Justice Anthony Kennedy, a Regan appointee, told the American Bar Association "I accept neither the wisdom, the justice, nor the necessity of mandatory minimums."[xxx]

In light of the backdoor of the sentencing guidelines, it should be of no shock to discover that the population in federal prison has quadrupled at a cost to tax payers of $4 billion per year. The concern with sentencing is not that crimes should go unpunished. The problem is that in some cases sentencing is unfair, and when it is unfair to one it could lead to unfairness for all.

An example of the heartless effect of sentencing was reported by CBSnews.com in 1991. Brenda Valencia, a 19 year old Miami resident, had never been in trouble with the law until she gave a ride to her roommate's stepmother. Brenda knew the woman was a drug dealer and knew that she was going to West Palm Beach to pick up money from a cocaine dealer. The federal drug Agents arrested Valencia, the woman she gave a ride to, and the two men who set up the deal. She was charged with being part of a cocaine conspiracy and the federal law required the judge to sentence her to at least 12 years and 7 months in prison, twice as many years as she would have gotten if she'd killed someone and been convicted of manslaughter.

The situation with Brenda Valencia is not an uncommon occurrence. I have represented many clients who were first time offenders of drug violations who received no less than a 15 year sentence. The effects of these laws are harsh and the evolution occurred suddenly, sparked by the notion of fear. The same notion of fear that caused our country to run into war with Iraq. The same notion of fear that has caused our civil liberties to be violated. The images of drug dealers roaming our streets, crack fiends walking into our homes and restaurants. Ramped violence and disruption caused the rush into these drug laws.

sentences rather than incarceration).

1	2	3	4	5	6	7	8	9
Community Population	Total: 250,000		White: 215,000 (86%)		Minority: 35,000 (14%)		Minority Percentage of Total Population Affected	Disparity Index (between current and previous stage of system)
Decision or Action	Total Population Affected by Action		White Population Affected by Action		Minority Population* Affected by Action			
	Number	Percent	Number	Percent	Number	Percent		
Arrest	25,000	10%	13,000	6.0%	12,000	34.0%	48%	3.4
Detain	5,000	20%	2,400	18.5%	2,600	21.7%	52%	1.1
Prosecute	23,750	95%	12,350	95.0%	11,400	95.0%	48%	1.0
Convict	14,250	60%	6,412	51.9%	7,838	68.8%	55%	1.2
Community Sentence	9,975	70%	5,115	79.8%	4,860	62.0%	49%	0.9
Incarcerate	4,275	30%	1,297	20.2%	2,978	38.0%	70%	1.3

* "Minority" refers to: African Americans, Latinos, Asians, Native Americans and other persons of color.

Figure 3
Current and Proposed Sentences
Of All Major Drug Trafficking Offenders
Fiscal Year 2000

Average Sentence (in months)

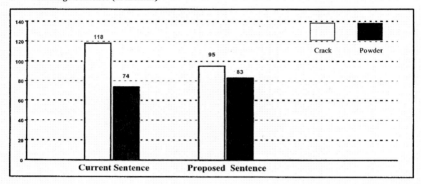

Assumes crack cocaine mandatory minimum of 25 grams and enhancements for weapons, bodily injury, prior drug felony, and importation (for powder and crack cocaine only).

SOURCE: U.S. Sentencing Commission, 2000 Datafile, USSCFY00 and the Commission's Prison Impact Model.

How to Get a Break - "substantial assistance," and the "Safety Valve."

A judge in a case involving a charge that carries a mandatory minimum sentence cannot ususally impose a sentence below that minimum. There is one exception, and it can only be requested by the Justice Department. The sole exception for a mandatory minimum sentence exists when the government says that a drug offender has given "substantial assistance" to the government in the prosecution of another drug offender. One of the common ways that the Justice Department gets testimony in drug cases is to offer to other drug offenders the possibility of a more lenient sentence if they testify the target. Section 5K1.1 of the U.S.

Sentencing Guidelines allows a judge to grant a lower sentence to a defendant whom the prosecutor says has given substantial assistance. Over the last 5 years nearly a third of the people sentenced in drug trafficking cases in the federal system had their sentences reduced under the substantial assistance provisions because they gave information on other people. This information can be based on the case that the person is involved with, or even by giving information on some other case and person.

	Number Total Cases	# Sub. Assistance Cases	%e of Total	Sub Ass. Average Month Sentence	Sub Ass. Average Month Departure	Average Percent Departure
All Offense	191,712	37,481	19.6	40.6	47.4	59.6
Drug Trafficking	76,584	24,608	32.1	52.3	60.5	54.7
Drug Trafficking, 10+ year minimum	28,912	11,829	40.9	80.8	94.8	54.2

Source – U.S. Sentencing Commission, 1993-1007 individual federal offenders

In the streets the person who gives information on another person, or that person's case is called a "snitch." Normally, this term "snitch" has a negative connotation, but the reality is that it happens in a large majority of cases. In fact, the average person who assists the government receives a sentence reduction of almost 50%.

So how does it work? A drug offender while in jail awaiting trial learn the names of other persons awaiting trial. He learns that he can easily make up a story that will get him out of prison if his story provides "substantial assistance" in the prosecution of someone else as a "high level trafficker." The quantity of drugs in a drug case need not be shown by physical evidence.

The availability of substantial assistance works because it only takes simple testimony of a witness to account for a person selling drugs, and the amounts of drugs that person sold. This testimony is enough to bring a case against the other individual that a quantity of drugs was sold. Accordingly, a clever informant can prove that someone else is a "high level trafficker" without too much trouble.

To Help Yourself or Not

The question becomes, should a person give assistance to the government to convict another person? That decision has to be made on an individual basis. I will state that if you are not involved in the situation and are somehow implicated, to tell that another person is truly the responsible individual may be the right thing to do. Let me give you an example. I had a client who was charged with multiple drug violations. The police officers searched her vehicle and found cocaine, PCP, marijuana, ecstasy, and guns. She was the only person in the vehicle, and she was asleep at the time she was approached by the police officers. The person who brought the drugs in town with her was gone. He fled from police and ultimately escaped. This young lady was caught with all of his drugs. To understand the situation you must have a profile of the young lady. She was in college at the time, a talented artist, musician, and at the age of 23 she had no criminal record. The guy she was with was in his thirties. Throughout my legal representation of this young lady, she maintained that she would not "snitch" on her boyfriend. Regardless of the fact that he did not post her bail, he did not pay her attorney fees, and he would not turn himself in, she felt that he was worth going to jail for. I must add that in Ohio, for the amount of drugs that she had, her potential sentence was from 2 to 30 years with at least 2 years mandatory time.

That is the attitude of old. In the times of Wayne Perry and John Gotti people would be "stand up guys" and not turn or "snitch" on each other, but in today's climate, more people decide to help themselves. The young lady I spoke about was in a situation that many people find themselves in; she was in love, and in the wrong situation. She knew her boyfriend was a drug dealer, and knew that drugs were in the vehicle she rented. What she failed to realize is that the Legal Matrix is real and once it has its grip on you there is no letting go. In her situation, the best decision would have been to forgo the "I'm gonna stick by my man" speech and help herself out of a harmful situation.

How the Legal Matrix will Take Your stuff - What are forfeiture laws?

Since 1970, the federal drug laws have allowed the government to seize property that is used in drug crimes or that results from the profit of drug crimes. When the government takes ownership of this seized property, it is called forfeiture. Logically, these laws make sense. People who own and use property like airplanes, and ships to smuggle drugs to the U.S. deserve to have those items taken away. Obviously, there is a dark side to the use and application of the forfeiture laws.

- These laws can be applied to property even when the owners are not accused of drug trafficking, even when the owners had no knowledge that the property was being used in drug trafficking.

- These laws can be applied even when the owner of the property takes steps to prevent the property from being used in drug trafficking, but has been unsuccessful.

Once the forfeiture laws take effect, the property owner is required to bring a lawsuit to get his/her property back. He or she must post a cash bond in order to bring the suit. If the property owner has no cash or no more valuable assets, they are not able to get their property back. If the property owner cannot afford a lawyer to bring the lawsuit, they cannot get their property back. In some jurisdictions, the laws require the lawsuit to be filed within 10 days of the seizure of the property. If you wait more than 10 days, for example, because you are trying to figure out if you need a lawyer or where you can find such a lawyer, then you lose the property even if you are completely innocent.

The proceeds of forfeited property go to the law enforcement agencies that make the seizures, not to the general federal treasury. Yes there is a formula that will detail the division of the proceeds between the prosecutors, law enforcement agencies and other funds, but the property, which is not sold, goes to the law enforcement agencies. This creates a powerful incentive to seize and forfeit property, even in unmerited cases. These laws are so offensive to justice that even the staunchest advocates of tough on crime policies like the conservative chairman of the House Judiciary Committee, Henry Hyde of Illinois, have called out for their reform.

Asset seizures by the Drug Enforcement Administration, fiscal year 1997

Type of Asset	Number of seizures	Value
Total	**15,860**	**$551,680,150**
Currency	8,123	284,680,029
Other financial instruments	507	73,602,092
Real property	748	108,833,498
Vehicles	3,695	47,379,874
Vessels	111	5,884,754
Aircraft	24	8,945,000
Other conveyance	172	1,734,731
Other	2,480	20,620,172

Source: Sourcebook of Criminal Justice Statistics 1997

The fact of the matter is that the practical application of the forfeiture laws forces people whose assets are seized to be treated as if they're guilty and they must prove themselves innocent to get their property back. One example of the problems of over aggressive forfeiture pursuits is a situation out of Morgan Hill, California. Carl and Mary Sheldon sold their home and agreed to carry a $160,000 note. They had no idea they were about to be trapped in a government web that would cost them almost everything they owned. In 1979, the Sheldon's made the mistake of selling their $289,000 house in Moraga, Calif., to a man later convicted under a federal law that permits the government to seize his property as the product of his ill-gotten gains. The fact that the Sheldon's had nothing to do with the crimes and were the legal owners', courtesy of the unpaid mortgage, meant nothing. After a 10-year court battle, they are virtually bankrupt. They got back the house, but it was so badly damaged that it made little difference.

The Sheldon's are not unique. Authorities across the nation are coming under fire from citizens whose homes, cars, cash and other property were seized in America's War on Drugs. Prosecutors and law enforcement officials insist the program, included in the Comprehensive Crime Control Act of 1984 and codified in many state laws, is helping them fight the drug war. They say the seizures hurt dealers where it counts-in the pocketbook.

As it has been noted by some news headlines, when given the opportunity, the use of forfeiture and seizures have been abused. For example:

- A small-town Southern sheriff seized a Rolls-Royce from a drug dealer and uses it as his personal car.

- Local police in Little Compton, Rhode Island, net $3.8 million in a drug bust and outfit their cars with $1,700 video cameras and heat detection devices for a police force of seven.

- The owner of a sailboat loses the craft after a crew member is caught with a small amount of marijuana.

- A prosecutor drives a confiscated BMW. Sheriffs fill their coffers with cash seized from motorists.

- People lose their homes because their kids sold drugs in the basement.

Another case involved Jorge Lovato Jr., a computer reseller in Morgan Hill, California., and Rey Sotelo, a motorcycle shop owner in nearby Gilroy. Of course we know that having previous drug convictions, and being once tied to a suspected drug dealer, garners very little sympathy from most people. Because of this fact, Agents raided Sotelo's home and both men's businesses, seizing company records and a Harley-Davidson motorcycle that was for sale on consignment at Sotelo's bike shop. They later seized $120,000 in cash from a safe-deposit box rented to Lovato. Police said they suspected the money was illegal drug proceeds, and that the motorcycle was stolen.

Neither Lovato nor Sotelo were charged with a crime. Lovato said he keeps large amounts of cash available because he deals in cash purchases. Lovato and Sotelo both think police targeted them because of their former ties with the key target in the raids of a man with whom they were partners in a failed export business. Five months and $10,000 in lawyers' fees later, Lovato got his money back.[xxxi]

In practice, the laws also aim to increase the cost of the crime. Someone who drives an expensive car into an area to buy drugs, for example, could end up losing the vehicle, even if the drug charge turns out to be minor. The problem we face, and a problem that is inherent in the Legal Matrix, is that the person isn't always guilty, yet even the innocent sometimes have great difficulty getting their property back. In addition, in many cases, public officials have been allowed to keep the assets for law-enforcement, or even for personal use. For example, within the first 5 years of the 6 year-old federal asset forfeiture program, the Justice Department confiscated $5.2 billion in cash and property, including many millions more shared with state agencies.

Other examples include minor offenders such as Dick Kaster, a retired foreman in Ventura, Iowa, whose $6,000 boat was taken away after he was convicted of illegally catching three fish. Not to mention the fact that sheriffs, police officers and federal Agents in several parts of the country have been accused of confiscating millions of dollars in cash by stopping mostly African Americans and Hispanic travelers whom they allege were drug money couriers, taking their money, and then releasing the travelers without filing charges. This situation happened in the City of East Cleveland when two female officers where accused of regularly "shaking down" drug dealers in the neighborhood. Then we wonder why no one trusts our police officers or trust the Legal Matrix.

A forfeiture case is something out of Lewis Carroll's "Alice in Wonderland, where the rule is punishment first, trial later." says Brenda Grantland, a defense attorney who represents a grass-roots organization called FEAR, which lobbies to change the laws. "Once the American public finds out what's been going on under their noses without them knowing about it, they are going to be horrified," said Brenda Grantland. Grantland and other critics say many of those abuses could be remedied by the government doing the following:

- Prohibiting confiscation before conviction;
- Requiring that the value of the property seized be proportional to the crime;
- The government should be required to prove that the property was linked to criminal activity based on a higher standard - preponderance of evidence or beyond a reasonable doubt - rather than the easier standard of probable cause. (Although prosecutors must prove guilt beyond a

reasonable doubt, civil forfeiture can occur
when there is probable cause to believe the
property was connected to a crime-a far less
rigorous standard).[xxxii]

Although designed as a weapon against major drug dealers, civil forfeiture laws have spawned frightening new police powers across the country - including the power to confiscate private property from innocent citizens whose only mistake is being at the wrong place at the wrong time. It cost Donald A. Regan of Montvale, New Jersey his 1986 Camaro, $40,000 in legal fees and much of his reputation. Regan had never heard of civil forfeiture when he allowed a customer at a bar where he worked to tag along on an errand into Manhattan. Regan's mistake was that he agreed to make a stop in a nearby neighborhood so his passenger could pick up some money he said he was owed. During the trek back to New Jersey, they were surrounded by agents of the Bergen County Narcotics Task Force who had been conducting the stakeout. When he first heard sirens, Regan figured he had been speeding. Then his passenger informed him that he had 16 vials of cocaine in his pocket-not money. Both Regan and his passenger were arrested on drug charges. After the passenger exonerated Regan of any knowledge of the drug deal, all charges against Regan were dismissed by the police-yet there was a catch: The authorities wouldn't return his car.[xxxiii]

As a tool of the Legal Matrix, forfeiture laws have proven to be an often used, lucrative, and damaging program in the system. It furthers the long time saying that you must be careful of what you do, who you do it with, and who your friends are. Otherwise, your property can be taken or tied up in years of litigation while you try to prove that you are a victim and not a criminal.

White Crime v. Black Crime

Yrs Per $Mil	Name/Company Sentencing Date	Charge /Crimes	Sentence	Their Gain from Crime
.06	Ivan Boesky / arbitrager / Dec.1987	Insider Trading	3 years	$50 million
.06	Reed Slatkin / investment advisor / Sept.2003	Swindled Investors	14 years	$240 million
1.4	Samuel Waksal / ImClone / June 2003	Fraud, Perjury	7 years	$5 million
2.3	Alan Bond / Albriond Capital Mgmt / Feb.2003	Swindled Investors	12.6 years	$5.5 million
3.3	Leona Helmsley / Helmsley Ent / Dec.1989	Income Tax Evasion	4 years	$1.2 million
3.9	Emery Harris / HealthSouth / Dec.2003	Inflated Earning	5 months	$106,500
4.5	Steve Madden / Steve Madden Ltd. / May 2002	Insider Trading	3.4 years	$784,000
50.9	Jamie Olis / Dynegy / March 2004	Securities Fraud	24	$472,000
11.5	Robert DiBlasi / Private citizen / Aug.1999	Stole AA batteries	31 yrs - life (3rd strike)	$2.69

The facts are real, the Sentencing guidelines affect African Americans and other minorities more harshly than non-minorities. Take for example the chart below; it's from an article called "Does Crime Pay?" *Forbes Magazine April 16, 2004.*

The result is that white collar criminals are less likely to go to jail for the serious crimes they commit, even though it is a known fact that the white collar criminals often cause more damage and harm than any other criminals. For instance, when a person is defrauded of their entire life savings due to some action by a corporate leader that is a serious crime. On the other hand, many people refer to drug crimes as "victimless crimes." They are called victimless because the person who uses the drugs do so at their own discretion and the people who sell the drugs do not force the users to use. I will not necessarily endorse the victimless crime position but I pose the following question. Is it fair that a drug dealer should get a life sentence for selling drugs when a corporate leader, who destroys the financial lives of millions, get a short prison sentence and then arrives back to their wonderful homes and privileged lifestyles? But then again even America's sweetheart, Martha Stewart, was forced to spend some time in jail. The Legal Matrix is unpredictable.

Understanding the Drug Game

Life With Your Back Against the Wall

The most common reason I hear in support of selling drugs is the **hopelessness** many inner city men and women feel about their economic situation. When investigated, it is determined that one source of this hopelessness stems from the visual reality of the inner city. The constant presence of violence, dirty and unsafe neighborhoods, poor economic and job opportunities give a negative outlook on the idea of a hard working man/woman. This is the environment that young inner city residents view, and live in everyday. Beyond just viewing these conditions, they live the conditions. Jobs are few, crime is rampant, and often the perception is that the only way to make money is to hustle drugs or some other illegal activity. Beyond being just a perception, when there are no jobs to be found, poor housing conditions, and bills to pay, this lifestyle goes beyond perception and becomes the reality.

On top of the inner city's depressed environment, we must add the fact that some of the most easily **identifiable successful people** in the neighborhood are the hustlers. They are the ones driving the nice cars, in the nicer homes and with the nice clothes. For all intents and purposes the hustler is living the American dream. Young people grow up with this exposure and wind up tempted to enter this industry.

> The fact that entrance into the drug trade is easier than getting a job speaks volumes for the reasons that many young people enter this industry.

Another reason I hear, in excuse for the drug trade, is the argument that the government planted crack and cocaine in the inner cities, thereby creating the monster that exists within the city. The question of the origins of drugs in America is a puzzling inquiry. One thing we know for sure is that cocaine is not produced in this country, so it must have come from another source. We also know the beginning of the cocaine and crack epidemic started on the West coast of this country. As I indicated early in this writing, I am not here to support or deny a particular theory, but I have come to believe that whether it was by negligence or chance, the fact remains that cocaine and crack made its way into the United States by some forces other than the thousands of African Americans and other people who use, sell, are charged and incarcerated for possessing or trafficking the drugs. My thoughts are that, if the government did not bring the drugs into this country, it is negligent in stopping the drugs from entering this country and spreading through the cities.

Drug Selling as a Career Opportunity

As I stated before, we cannot forget or disregard the influence of the environment itself. The fact that entrance into the drug trade is easier than getting a job speaks volumes for the reasons that many young people enter this industry. Whether the drugs were planted in the inner cities or not does nothing to take away the fact that today, it is easier to sell drugs than to involve yourself in productive positive activities. There are more drug dealers in the community than opportunities.

How Parents Influence

So if we discount and get rid of the conspiracy theory, I believe another pressing issue and reason why inner city residents seem to gravitate to drug dealings is the lack of positive parental influence. Here are the most common situations:

1. Either the mother or father is **too busy working** to properly inform and raise the child,
2. the parents **are not working** and not **educated** enough to inform the child, or the parent is **strung out** on drugs themselves,
3. there is only one parent or no parent in the home (child being raised by grandmother or other relative), and too busy to carefully watch and monitor the children's actions.
4. The child makes up his or her mind to do the wrong thing.

If there was some type of realistic accountability from the home, many drug dealers would be forced to find another way to raise money.

I have a personal understanding of the mistakes and situations that lead to involvement in the drug game. How could I not understand? I am from the inner city, the ghetto. I lived in the environment, and I fell into the trap of dealing drugs. My story, in some respects, is similar to many, and at the same time, very different. I was raised by a single mother. Later my mother had a boyfriend move into the home, but the relationship was not one of a father figure. Instead, it was tumultuous because he was not my father. My mother was often pitted between the two of us. Although she never made him leave the house, she made sure I understood that I was the most important part of her life and that she would always take care of me, but that did not stop me. The lure of the streets, the temptation grabbed me.

I also had an older brother who was a graduating high school senior when I was born. He was very influential in my later development, but in the early years he became a father figure, but that was not enough. The environment of East Cleveland at that time was terrible; however, it was not too far removed from African American's who could remember the neighborhood being all White Americans and "all good." My mother remembered being among the first African Americans to live in the city and on that particular street. I must admit that I did not truly appreciate how poor I was. It was not until junior high when I bargained for a used leather jacket and in high school, when I would ask a friend to let me wear his jewelry that I realized there were many things I did not have. Unlike most of the youth today, my brother was active as a father figure and he was a successful student and professional. He constantly influenced my desire for finer things and stressed to me that through education and hard work I could obtain anything. My mother backed this sentiment up with words and support, at least in the best way she could.

The bug hit me when I was in high school. I no longer wanted to be the young man without the nice clothes, the latest tennis shoes, the jewelry and the car. I made a decision to sell drugs even though everything in my upbringing indicated that it was a bad thing to do. I was a true ghetto aberration in the sense that I had a mother pushing me in the right direction and a very successful brother, yet I still decided to go the route of the streets.

I remember like it was yesterday, I begged a friend to let me get involved, to let me deliver his drugs, and I did it for free. That was my start. Where was my mother during all this? Like most inner city single mothers, she was working all day and tired at night. So I began to sneak and learn the trade, build my business and became "successful." Throughout the ordeal, my life was threatened by words, physical violence and close encounters with the police. I lived the life of a drug dealer while being successful in school, a leader, and a college bound student. I continued this life while pursuing a finance degree in college. I continued this business while working for a Fortune 500 company, and while applying to law school. I stopped selling drugs the very day my mother passed away.

I learned a lot from my dealings, but most important to this text, I learned every reason why not to get involved in it. The game is serious, but unfortunately, though it called a game, it is not. There are brushes with death. Death through physical violence, death through incarceration and death through the detiriation of your soul.

I am not proud of my past activity, but I know it created the person I am today; the awareness, the identification with my community, its temptations, and problems. I have the insight to guide the next generation through the Legal Matrix. Most importantly, I am able to use the experiences of my past to be an Oracle or source of information for others behind me; those who can not see past the reality of the ghetto, those determined to do the wrong thing. Now that we understand the environment and the reason so many inner city people fall into the trap of drug selling, we must now turn our focus to providing a way out of this trap of the Legal Matrix.

The View from the Man in the Streets

The man in the street approaches most activities, and situations from the viewpoint of his own knowledge. There is a strong saying that you can not see beyond that which you don't understand. That being said, the man in the street, often, does not see beyond the inner city environment. When you wake up in the morning and see struggle in your neighborhood, countered with opulence on television, you see despair in the hood, compared to happiness on the television. You see dead end situations in the hood, compared with the endless opportunities available to others. Your reality can fuel the acceptance of illegal means to achieve your goals.

I have often wondered why adults who know the system, or have at least been exposed to the system, would continue to sell drugs and conduct illegal activities. The answer is obvious, but disturbing. Many feel there is no other way to reach their financial goals. The financial goal, the desire to live a certain lifestyle, is what pushes people to the extent of selling drugs for a living. Then you have those who got caught in the drug trade, become convicted felons, and now find it is very hard to get meaningful employment. The problem is most of the convicted felons are not really looking for meaningful employment; they are simply looking for a way to maintain certain lifestyle expectations.

ACTIVITY	DESIRE	RISK	RESULT
Selling Crack	Money Cars Popularity Women	Jail –6 months to – 10 years to life	Jail for life: Can not provide for anyone, not children or family. Independence and freedom no longer.
Stealing/robbery	Money Material Possessions	Min 90 days to 10 years	How you obtain riches is likely how you will lose it.
Gang Activity	Friendship Money	Death, Jail	No association is worth losing your respect, independence, family or life.

Inner City Citizens are Targeted

Why are there so many inner city people caught in the Legal Matrix? The answer is that the inner city inhabitants are specific targets of the Legal Matrix. But understand, being targeted is not an excuse. When you take the risk and involve yourself in illegal activities the law and the Legal Matrix will come down on you. People talk about it all the time, but I don't believe there is any real thought given to the truth of that assertion. If you know you may be a target to be robbed (on a certain day, in a certain way and in a certain neighborhood) wouldn't you change the way you conduct your activities? Most people would. So one of the only conclusions that I can make, other than that one expressed above is that there is no true acknowledgement that the inner city is a target. If people understood this, there would be no dealing in drugs or not as much.

Nearly 90 percent of the offenders convicted in federal court for crack-cocaine distribution are African-American while the majority of crack-cocaine users are white.

If you need a true example, just look at the following summary of the federal sentencing guidelines when it comes to offenses involving drugs.

COCAINE AMOUNT	CRACK AMOUNT	SENTENCE
150 Kilos of Cocaine	1.5 Kilos of Crack Cocaine	From as little as 19.5 years to as much as **Life** in prison
50 – 150 Kilos of Cocaine	500 grams to 1.5 Kilos of Crack Cocaine	From as little as 15.6 years to 33 years in prison
2-3.5 Kilos of Cocaine	20 – 35 grams of Crack Cocaine	From as little as 6.5 years to as much as 14.5 in prison

As the chart above shows, a man who owns and controls a warehouse with about 150 or more kilograms of pure cocaine, a person who obviously has strong connections with a source of larger supplies of cocaine, will get the exact same sentence as a young man who has possession of just 1 ½ kilograms of crack cocaine. The irony of this sentencing disparity is that fact that the former person, the one with the warehouse, knows that he/she is a major part of a large drug business worth billions of dollars, whereas the person with the 1 ½ kilograms of Crack probably thinks that he is a "big shot" based on the amount of money he is making. In reality he/she is in no comparison a "big shot," but will be treated worse than one, treated as a "king pin" if he is caught with that product.

Risk v. Reward

On the surface it would appear that the risk is easy to identify. You get involved with drugs and you end up in jail or dead. The truth is, the risk is not that clear. There are hidden risks most young men and women are not familiar with. In fact, I think the main problem is that most people who begin selling drugs don't even think about the risks. I didn't.

The obvious risks are losing money, getting ripped off, or the possibility of death. The, not so obvious risk is the fact that your liberties can be taken away for a very long time. Understanding that your liberty can be taken away in the name of mandatory minimums and the fact that drug offenses are treated as worse crimes then many others, the risk totally outweighs the reward. The graph below shows how the Legal Matrix is attacking very specific activities. This in turn becomes an attack on specific persons and places.

OFFENSE	MONTHS IN PRISON
Drug Trafficking	82.3
Sexual Abuse	73.3
Assault	38.8
Manslaughter	34.2
Bribery	22.9

What is the crack cocaine vs. powder cocaine disparity?

Pharmacologically the same drug, crack cocaine and powder cocaine are treated very differently within the walls of our justice system. Current policy generates a 100 to 1 penalty ratio for crack-related offenses. For instance, possession of only 5 grams of crack-cocaine yields a 5 year mandatory minimum sentence, however it takes <u>500 grams of powder cocaine</u> to prompt the same sentence. Moreover, crack-cocaine is the only drug for which the first offense of simple possession can trigger a federal mandatory minimum sentence. Yet "simple possession of any quantity of any other controlled substance by a first time offender - including powder cocaine – can be a misdemeanor offense punishable by a maximum of one year in prison." (21 U.S.C. 844).

In 1995, the U.S. Sentencing Commission recommended a more equitable ratio between crack and powder cocaine. However, Congress discarded the Commission's request and President Clinton signed the rejection into law. This marked the first occasion that Congress rejected a recommendation by the Sentencing Commission. Since then, the USSC has recommended reducing the disparity on several occasions to at least 20:1.

How does the Crack vs. powder cocaine disparity Affect Us?

The crack/powder disparity fuels drug war racial injustice. A report published by the U.S. Sentencing Commission notes that nearly 90 percent of the offenders convicted in federal court for crack-cocaine distribution are African American while the majority of crack-cocaine users are White Americans. The report concludes that "sentences appear to be harsher and more severe for racial minorities than others as a result of this law. The current penalty structure results in a perception of unfairness and inconsistency."

Much conversation about the disparity in sentencing has led to no action. In order to defeat the Legal Matrix, we must fight until the end, using every resource available to achieve our goal of freedom. In fact, on a local level, In the State of New York, Russell Simmons took a strong stand, against the Rockefeller Drug Laws that have a similar effect of imposing steeper penalties on drug activities that take place mainly in inner city communities.

The sentencing laws speak for themselves, the inner city citizens are clear targets when it comes to the drug trade. There is no other way to put it. Add to the sentencing guidelines the fact that there are more police patrolling the inner cities than there are police patrolling the borders. There are police in the inner cities who conduct corrupt activities, and practices to catch the low level criminals, compared with virtually no presence of major law enforcement harassing the true drug king pins. The inner city is a target and the inner city hustler will definitely, at some point, be caught by the Legal Matrix.

How Can the Legal Matrix Drug Laws Be Changed

1. *Allow judges to determine whether a specific drug case should be handled more appropriately by state, local or federal courts.*

The federal government has developed a national criminal code that results in many cases being handled by federal courts which should be handled by local courts. With regard to drug prosecution, the power of federal prosecutors has been so greatly increased that prosecutors play a larger role in administering justice than judges in drug cases. Federal judges can be given some control over justice in drug cases by giving them the authority to issue a pretrial ruling that allows them to remand a case to the local courts. Judges can weigh whether the offenses charged are more locally based, whether local courts are better able to evaluate the circumstances of an individual defendant, or whether a local drug court would be more appropriate for the offender. As an alternative, the Department of Justice could develop guidelines which reduce the number of inappropriate prosecutions they undertake.

Local courts, which have the ability to be more connected with the alleged criminal, can possibly make better decisions regarding how to charge, sentence, or otherwise dispose of the case.

2. *End the disparity between crack and powder cocaine sentencing.*

As we have discussed, the sentencing disparity between crack and powder cocaine has wreaked havoc on minority communities. The powder form of cocaine which is preferred by wealthier (usually White) consumers, requires 100 times as much weight to trigger the same penalty as the crack form. These stiff penalties apply to the mere possession of crack, unlike any other drug which requires an intent to distribute. As an initial step to address this blatant inequity, the penalties for these two forms of the same drug should be harmonized at the current levels for powder cocaine.

In 1986, before mandatory minimums instituted the crack/powder sentencing disparity, the average sentence for African Americans was 6% longer than the average sentence for White Americans. 4 years later following the implementation of this law, the average sentence was 93% higher for African Americans. Furthermore this overly harsh approach encourages drug dealers to enlist young children in their trade in an effort to escape prosecution.

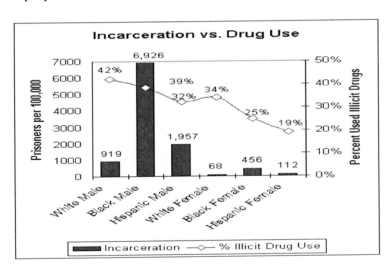

Today, 1 in 4 African American men can expect to be incarcerated in his lifetime. This widespread incarceration of African American males has increased the burdens on the African American family unit, as well as the entire community. Our drug laws should not fall disproportionately on one ethnic group. This disparity undermines efforts to stabilize communities, and reduce the impact of drug use and abuse.

The drug war has succeeded in arresting, and incarcerating large numbers of people. As of June 1996, 5.5 million Americans were under some form of control by the justice system. This translates into 1 out of every 35 adults in the nation. (Bureau of Justice Statistics. (1997, August 14). *Nation's probation and parole population reached almost 3.9 million last year.* Press Release. Washington, DC: Department of Justice).

3. *Restore civil liberties and individual rights undermined by current drug policies.*

Throughout the last two decades of the drug war, Congress and the courts have allowed a massive erosion of long-term, fundamental civil liberties. The warning of Justices William Brennan and Thurgood Marshall has come true: "…the first and worst casualty of the War on Drugs will be the precious liberties of our citizens."

As the United States moves to a public health-based drug control strategy, it should restore constitutional protection for individual rights. Among the drug war decisions that need to be reconsidered by the courts or for which legislation is needed are those which:

- Stop allowing police to stop and detain travelers in airports merely because they fit a 'drug courier profile' without a search warrant or any evidence that the individual committed a crime. Currently, a person can be legally detained if he or she is carrying heavy luggage, is young, is casually dressed, is nervous, pays cash for a ticket, and leaves his or her address off of the luggage.

- Stop allowing dogs to sniff travelers' luggage without probable cause.

- Stop allowing schools to drug test students without probable cause or warrant.

- Stop allowing police to search automobiles and containers in glove compartments (e.g., brief cases, trunks) without a search warrant.

- Stop allowing electronic surveillance of vehicles without a search warrant.

- Stop allowing police to search homes based on an anonymous tip from an unnamed informant.

- Stop allowing police to ignore "no trespassing" signs to search private property without a warrant or any probable cause that a crime has been committed.[xxxiv]

- Stop allowing police to search barns and other buildings adjacent to a residence without a warrant or any probable cause that a crime has been committed.[xxxv]

- Stop allowing police to search private property through aerial surveillance without a search warrant or any probable cause that a crime has been committed.[xxxvi]

- Stop allowing police to search bank records without the consent of the customer.[xxxvii]

- Stop allowing police to record telephone numbers dialed from one's home without the consent of the subscriber.[xxxviii]

- Stop allowing police to tape record telephone or face-to-face communications without the consent of the party being recorded and without a search warrant.[xxxix]

- Stop allowing police to search materials in a person's trash bag without a warrant or probable cause that a crime has been committed.[xl]

- Stop allowing police to instruct the United States Postal Service to record the return address and other information on the outside of a person's incoming mail without a warrant or even probable cause.

Drugs Are Addictive, So is Drug Dealing

The addiction to the drug game is easy to understand. The money, the cars, the women, the ghetto fame. By ghetto fame I mean, the drug dealer being a popular and respected person in the community. As I said earlier, drug dealers are often considered the only successful people in the community. I was addicted and it took a long time for me to get out of the game. I had every good reason to let it go - education, family, and career. I just could not stop. It was an obsession and I was in deep. Only my relationship with the Lord, which was brought into perspective after the death of my mother, caused me to stop my destructive behavior.

The addiction to the drug game runs deep. After experiencing the cash flow and being able to plan and set goals based on these expectations, it is hard to give up the fast cash. It is also difficult to fill the void that is created by the "hustler spirit." The hustler spirit is the feeling that goes with trying to make the best of your situation and win against the most difficult odds. I was smart enough to recognize that this same quality, the drive and the "hustler spirit" are the same qualities that are required to succeed in life. It is more useful and productive to apply this practice to a legal activity that will keep us successful in the Legal Matrix and not a victim of it.

Drugs Provide a Temporary Cure for Hopelessness, So Does Selling Drugs

I lived in the ghetto. My mother, rest her soul, did her best to provide for me, but there were times when we ate cereal for dinner, not because we wanted to but we had to. There were times when we also had to go without other necessities. To her credit, we never had nights without heat or electricity, but it was hard on her. I remember she bought me a VCR for Christmas; it took her 5 years to pay the VCR off (to this day, when I see the commercial for the store that sold her the VCR at those high interest rates, I get disturbed). I had a lot of friends, but I know the feeling of hopelessness, wondering if you can make it out of the ghetto and experience the life you see on television.

This hopelessness is the feeling that breeds temptation to act outside the law and risk being caught in the Legal Matrix. When a person believes his or her situation is hopeless there are no limits to how they may act. It was said best by late rapper/actor Tupac Shakur, "People are hungry and are outside the door knowing that people with food are on the other side. First the hungry will knock on the door and ask for the food, next they will attempt to convince the others to give them the food, and eventually they will knock down the door and take the food." This is the plight of the hopeless mentality.

The problem with the hopeless mentality is the lack of vision. For the most part, no situation is completely hopeless. No situation is so hopeless that we should be willing to give up our freedom. If there is concern about caring and providing for your family, think about how hard it will be for you to provide for your family if you are in jail. If you are concerned about the ability to pay rent, think about how difficult it will be to pay rent if you are dead. The bottom line is that being caught in the Legal Matrix, having your liberty taken away is the ultimate situation of lost hope. By avoiding the Legal Matrix, we still have the option of freedom, and choices.

Instead of focusing on the hopelessness, I focused on the opportunities. No matter how bad you think the situation is, there is an opportunity to better your life and to choose a different path to get out of the ghetto. That's what I decided to do.

Here is your way out of the Drug Life Regardless of the Laws, we have a Choice

1.   Know the risks

If you are going to make a decision that has the potential to change your life, why not know all the facts. The thoughtlessness that goes into selling and using drugs is comparable to how many young people approach parenthood. Many people just jump into the situation without thinking about the future, the risks, the pitfalls and the consequences. It is senseless to undertake the risks of the Legal Matrix without first trying to figure it out. Why are certain laws designed in certain ways? Why are some people spending extremely long periods of time behind bars? Ask why, and then find out. In other words, look before you leap.

I have many friends and acquaintances, who would rather make a million dollars in exchange for time behind bars. They actually believe that jail is no big deal. This point of view is short sighted at best. If you think about the future of your community, your family, and your own future, you will see that hustling is not the best way. People talk about putting food on their child's dinner table and clothes on the children's back. Ask these same people who will provide for their children when they're locked up in jail, or dead. I would ask them if their children's life is more enriched by the ability of the child to wear the latest clothes, and best shoes when there is a strong possibility that they will eventually have to visit their parent in jail, or worse, grow up without a parent at all. Would it not be better for that same child to watch his parent go to work everyday rather than to be forced to visit their parent behind bars?

2.   Make the choice to have a better life.

A better life comes from refining and polishing your skills. It takes a lot of street smarts to learn, and succeed at a hustle. It also takes a lot of concentration and planning to elude the police time and time again. These same skills can be used to succeed in business. The street entrepreneurs can mold and polish these skills so they can come out of the inner cities, creating jobs, motivating young people, and strengthening the community. It's about choice.

3.   Pass your knowledge and experience on to younger generations.

Become Oracles, tell your war stories, and help keep younger people from making the same mistakes that you made. Tell about the traps you where unaware of. I often speak about drug life, and other ills of the inner city. On a specific occasion, I asked a woman her opinion as to why so many young women are willing to have children as single mothers. The result of our conversation was that we are not truly active in informing our young people of the risks, and circumstances they face and expose themselves to when they make critical decisions without careful thought. At some point it will be up to all of us to inform those without knowledge about the truth. It will be up to us to help "free" the minds of those who are unaware. Take the time to approach a young man selling drugs, and give him the right information. Step into the lives of people who are lost and hurting, it's our duty. When we teach we learn.

4.   Recognize your blessings

Be happy with the blessings you have. Most of my practice as a criminal attorney includes keeping individuals out of jail. Although I truly enjoy helping people keep their liberties, the bad part is that many people do not learn from their mistakes. I make it a point to tell my clients that beating the case has given you a new lease on life. It is not that you are untouchable, but at this particular time, the Legal Matrix did not get you. Look at the situation as a stepping stone to cleaning up mistake and living right. There is something more in store for you. Don't keep making the same mistakes. It took me a long time to come to the point where I realized you don't have to be a millionaire to be happy. In fact, most people will never be a financial millionaire, but as long as you can support yourself and your family, live a lifestyle that will give you peace of mind whether you believe it or not, you will have the true riches.

The Program - The Patriot Act

"Experience should teach us to be most on our guard to protect liberty when the government's purposes are Beneficent. Men born to freedom are naturally alert to repel invasion of their liberty by evil minded rulers. The greatest dangers to liberty lurk in insidious encroachment by men of zeal, well-meaning but without understanding."
- Supreme Court Justice Louis Brandeis, in the case of *Olmsted v. United States.*[xli]

On October 26, 2001, President George W. Bush signed the Patriot Act (USAPA) into law. This law is the grandfather of all the Legal Matrix's programs. This law was passed just six weeks after

> I do not question the need to be safe in this country and to protect us from terrorism, but through the Patriot Act, the Legal Matrix is in full effect.

the attacks of September 11, 2001, which paralyzed our nation in fear and sorrow. The acronym stands for Uniting and Strengthening America by Providing Appropriate Tools Required to Intercept and Obstruct Terrorism Act. With this law domestic law enforcement and international intelligence agencies have been given a wide variety of new powers. In addition to the new powers many of the checks and balances that were provided by the American courts, to ensure our civil liberties are protected, were eliminated. Most of these checks and balances were put into place after previous accounts of misuse of surveillance powers by these same agencies, including the revelation in 1974 that the FBI and foreign intelligence agencies had spied on over 10,000 U.S. citizens, including Dr. Martin Luther King Jr.

The bill is 342 pages long, and it made changes to several different statutes. It's the fact that the USAPA made changes to other existing statutes that makes it very difficult for the average citizen to follow and determine to what extent their civil liberties have been changed or eliminated. The main Agents responsible for its passage are the people in the United States Department of Justice and Attorney General John Ashcroft. As I noted before, there are Agents that work for us and those who work against us. It is my belief that the Agents who work on our behalf were not aware of the details of this sweeping legislation. Due to the hysteria of the 9/11 attacks, there was not much debate about the law before its passage. As I said before, there are programs that work for us and those that work against us. This program, although its intentions are understood, overwhelmingly works against us, especially if we look at the possible long term effects. Below is a review of two controversial provisions of the act.

The "Material Support" Clause

One of the critical provisions of the new war on terrorism is the targeting of those who provide "material support" to terrorist organizations. The federal law now makes it both a crime and a deportable offense to provide "material support" to terrorist organizations. The danger of the "material support" standard is that it does not require a finding or proof that an individual intended to further terrorist activity. Instead, "material support" means providing physical assets, personnel, training or expert advice and assistance to a "designated" terrorist organization. *18 USCAa 2339B.* As noted by David Cole in *Lost Liberties,* "If this law had been on the books in the 1980s, the thousands of Americans who donated money to the African National Congress (ANC) for its lawful political struggle against apartheid would face lengthy prison terms because during those years the ANC was designated as a terrorist organization by our State Department."

So now we must be very careful what we do and who we do it with, otherwise we can find ourselves charged with materially supporting an activity that we did not even know existed.

The "Enemy Combatant" Designation

Another danger is the fact that the U.S. government is now able to invoke its military authority to bypass the normal and expected criminal process. This assertion of authority will not be reviewed by courts and they can use it to detain in military custody any person whom the president identifies as an "enemy combatant." As we know, soon after the attacks of 9/11 took place, Muslims and Arabs were designated as enemies. More than a thousand Muslims have been targeted, arrested and detained for weeks based on their religion and ethnicity. Notably most of these people have not been charged with a terrorist crime related to the September 11 attacks.

Now we must be careful to watch how we speak to people, who we speak about and what we say. The risk of being called an enemy combatant will likely censor many normal activities that we use to take for granted.

Why Should We Care about the Patriot Act?

> The government has been using the expanded powers of the Patriot Act to investigate suspected drug traffickers, white-collar criminals, blackmailers, child pornographers, money launderers, spies and even corrupt foreign leaders.

New Actions against gang members

It was reported in August of 2005 that Federal authorities arrested 582 alleged gang members over a two-week period, targeting an estimated 80 violent groups they say have spawned street crimes across the country. Homeland Security Secretary Michael Chertoff called the gangs "a threat to our homeland security and ... a very urgent law enforcement priority."[xlii]

The crackdown is part of ICE's ongoing "Operation Community Shield" campaign, targeting gang activity with other federal and state authorities. So far, ICE has made 1,057 arrests as part of the sting. Though the Investigators targeted members in 27 states of what they considered to be the most violent street gangs, including Mara Salvatrucha, or MS-13; Sure Inos; the 18th Street Gang; Latin Kings; the Mexican Mafia; Border Brothers; Brown Pride and numerous others, the fact is that once these laws are on the books, once they are a part of the Legal Matrix, the spiral begins.

Whether you realize it or not, the push for Homeland Security and the programs or laws that encompass the Patriot Act have truly jeopardized our protections under the Bill of Rights. Here is the attack:

- Under the **First Amendment** our freedom of speech, political association, religion and the press is under attack.

- Under the **Fourth Amendment,** our protection against unreasonable searches and seizures is under attack.

- Under the **Fifth Amendment,** our guarantees of due process and equal protections are limited.

- Under the **Sixth Amendment,** our guarantee to fair and speedy trials and the ability to confront witnesses are in danger.

What do these things mean in the context of the Legal Matrix? Well as we know, the system is designed to control us, therefore, the Patriot Act and other terrorism laws are in effect another mechanism of control.

The problem with these expanded rights is that under the Patriot Act the normal **Fourth Amendment** protections are eliminated. For example, when surveillance is done for regular law enforcement purposes, the probable cause standard of the **Fourth Amendment** applies to interception orders and search warrants. However, a court order compelling an internet service

142

provider to produce e-mail logs and addresses use a lower standard. Instead of probable cause, the government must only show "specific and articulable" facts showing "reasonable grounds to believe" that the records or information are relevant and material to an ongoing criminal investigation. The pen/trap order uses an even lower standard whereas the government need only tell the court that the surveillance is relevant to a criminal investigation.

I do not question the need to be safe in this country and to protect us from terrorism, but the Legal Matrix is in full effect in relation to the Patriot Act. The possibility to be arrested based on providing "material support" to a group labeled as a terrorist organization opens us all to prosecution. For instance, if the Nation of Islam is labeled as a terrorist organization and you, an average citizen in any of the inner cities in America, purchase a "Final Call" newspaper; will you be arrested for providing "material support" for your donation of $1 to the group? That is a problem. Through laws such as these, the Legal Matrix is growing and growing. Additionally, the fact that a person can be labeled as an "enemy combatant" and then arrested and detained without access to a lawyer causes serious problems. Any person who values freedom and the ability to defend ones self would be outraged by such authority. Any of us can disappear and be held as an "enemy combatant" and neither our family nor friends would have any idea where we are. How can you become labeled as an "enemy combatant," or as a person providing "material support?" Well that possibly exists through the use of a **"sneak and peak"** search of your home or a **roving phone tap.** Through the use of these innovative laws, the government can enter your home, "sneak and peak" around, copy your computer files and leave without giving you any notice. If that is not enough, the government can obtain a revolving phone tap that can intercept your conversation on any phone you have used or you are associated with.

The "Sneak and Peak" warrants allow the law enforcement agents to delay giving notice when they conduct a search. These actions are not stricken to terrorists' activities but also any criminal investigation. This is similar if not exactly like the "general writ of assistance" used by the British to search and seize whatever they wanted in the colonists' homes and businesses. These warrants make life in the Legal Matrix very difficult. Now, more than ever, our associations can lead to governmental investigation. In addition to the "Sneak and Peak," the "Magic Lantern", a devise that is attached to a computer and records every keystroke made, can be used to further invade our privacy.

Increased Surveillance Powers under the Patriot Act

Generally, the authorities of the Legal Matrix have greater surveillance powers and authority. Here is a review.

1.   **Internet Surveillance** – The government may spy on your web surfing which includes your search engine entries. To get this permission the government must simply tell a judge, anywhere in the U.S., that the spying could lead to information that is *"relevant"* to an ongoing criminal investigation.

2.   **Internet Account Information** – The USAPA allows Internet Service Providers (ISPs) to voluntarily hand over all "non-content" information to law enforcement with no need for any court order or subpoena. Furthermore, it expands the records that the government may seek with a simple subpoena (no court review required) to include records of session times and durations, temporarily assigned network addresses, the source of payments with the credit card or bank account numbers.

3. **Wiretaps** – The FBI and CIA can now go from phone to phone, computer to computer without demonstrating that each is even being used by a suspect or target of the order. Additionally, the government may now serve a wiretap, Foreign Intelligence Surveillance Act wiretap or pen/trap order on any person or entity nationwide, regardless of whether that person or entity is named in the order.

In addition to these increased surveillance and spying abilities, another shocking fact is that the government does not have to tell the courts or anyone what was discovered. As mentioned earlier, the government may generally spy on any individual who is thought to be a part of a terrorist group, participating in terrorist activity or even associating with such persons. The question is, who defines these people? Answer - The Legal Matrix.

Provisions of the Patriot Act

Domestic Law Enforcement Authority	Foreign Intelligence Surveillance Authority
1. Intercept Orders.	*1. FISA Intercept Orders.*
Title III (named after the section of the original legislation, the Omnibus Crime Control and Safe Streets Act of 1968) surveillance is a traditional wiretap that allows the police to bug rooms, listen to telephone conversations, or get content of electronic communications in real time.	• Secret Court. No public information about what surveillance requested or what surveillance actually occurs, except for a raw annual report of number of requests made and number granted (the secret court has only refused one request)
• Obtained after law enforcement makes a showing to a court that there is "probable cause" to believe that the target of the surveillance committed one of a special list of severe crimes.	• Previous standard was certification by Attorney General that "the purpose" of an order is a suspicion that the target is a foreign power or an agent of a foreign power.
• Law enforcement must report back to the court what it discovers.	• Attorney General is not required to report to the court what it does.
• Up to 30 days; must go back to court for 30-day extensions	• Up to 90 days, or 1 year (if foreign power)
(Courts do not treat unopened e-	

mail at ISPs as real-time communications.)	
2. Pen/Trap. Pen/Trap surveillance was based upon the physical wiring of the telephone system. It allowed law enforcement to obtain the telephone numbers of all calls made to or from a specific phone. • Allowed upon a "certification" to the court that the information is relevant to an ongoing criminal investigation. • Court must grant if proper application made • Does not require that the target be a suspect in that investigation and law enforcement is not required to report back to the court. Prior to USAPA there had been debate about how this is to be applied in the Internet context.	*2. FISA Pen/Trap.* Previous FISA pen/trap law required not only showing of relevance but also showing that the communications device had been used to contact an "agent of a foreign power." While this exceeds the showing under the ordinary pen/trap statute, such a showing had function of protecting US persons against FISA pen/trap surveillance.
3. Physical search warrants Judicial finding of probable cause of criminality; return on warrant. Previously, agents were required at the time of the	*3. FISA Physical search warrants* See FISA 50 USC § 1822. USAPA extends duration of physical searches. Under previous FISA, Attorney

search or soon thereafter to notify person whose premises were searched that search occurred, usually by leaving copy of warrant. USAPA makes it easier to obtain surreptitious or "sneak-and-peek" warrants under which notice can be delayed.	General (without court order) could authorize physical searches for up to one year of premises used exclusively by a foreign power if unlikely that US person will be searched; minimization required. A.G. could authorize such searches up to 45 days after judicial finding of probable cause that US target is or is an agent of a foreign power.
4. Subpoenas for stored information. Many statutes authorize subpoenas; grand juries may issue subpoenas as well. EFF's main concern here has been for stored electronic information, both e-mail communications and subscriber or transactional records held by ISPs. governed by the Electronic Communications Privacy Act (ECPA).	*4. FISA subpoenas* Previously, FISA authorized collection of business records in very limited situations, mainly records relating to common carriers, vehicles or travel, and only via court order. USAPA permits all "tangible things," including business records, to be obtained via a subpoena (no court order).
Domestic Law Enforcement	**Foreign Intelligence Surveillance**

New Definitions Under the Patriot Act

The USAPA expands the definition of Domestic Terrorism to include certain protest activities when violence breaks out. This can be considered an unfair standard when, often times, the out break of violence was not necessarily planned or expected. The act also exposes more people to surveillance through definitions of "harboring," and "support material."

Here are some details of a few of the previously mentioned provisions that we must all be aware of:

- **Law enforcement intercept orders (Wiretaps)**

  Wiretaps (for telephone conversations) can only be issued for certain crimes listed in 18 USC §2516. The Patriot Act adds to this list with **Terrorism** as a specific crime. (Note: this is probably redundant since the list already included most if not all terrorist acts --e.g., murder, hijacking, kidnapping, etc.)

- **Removes voicemail from Title III purview.**

  USAPA § 209 allows police to get voicemail and other stored wire communications without an intercept order; now, only a search warrant is needed.

- **"Sneak-and-peek" warrants greatly expanded.**

  Under USAPA § 213, the government can delay notification for "a reasonable period" which can be "extended for good cause shown" any wire or electronic communication listened to or tangible property taken. This is problematic because under our constitution, notice to a searched person is a key component of the Fourth Amendment reasonableness standard.

- **Law enforcement Pen/Trap orders**

  Pen/trap orders are issued by a court under a very low standard; the Patriot Act does not change this standard. Instead, it expands the reach of pen/trap orders to include internet information. USAPA § 216 modifies 18 USC § 3121(c) to expressly include routing, addressing information, thus expressly including e-mail and electronic communications. "Contents" of communications are excluded, but USAPA does not define what it includes (dialing, routing, addressing, signaling information) or what it excludes (contents). Serious questions exist about treatment of Web "addresses" and other web site locations that identify particular individuals. It is important to note that this provision does not "sunset" (it does not expire).

  Previously, pen/trap orders were limited by a court's jurisdiction, so they had to be installed in a specific judicial district. Now, courts shall enter ex parte order authorizing use anywhere within the United States if the court has jurisdiction over the crime being investigated and the attorney for U.S. Government has certified that information "likely to be obtained" is "relevant to an ongoing criminal investigation." The order applies to any provider "whose assistance may facilitate the execution of the order," whether or not within the jurisdiction of the issuing court. This is another provision that does not sunset. As a side bar, if the government agency uses its own technology (e.g., Carnivore), then an "audit trail" is required, e.g., 30 day report back to court.

- **Intercept orders: adds "roving wiretap" authority to FISA.**

USAPA §206 amends 50 USC §1805. Courts now may authorize intercepts on any phones, or computers that the target may use. Additionally, the foreign intelligence authorities can require anyone to help them wiretap. Previously they could only serve such orders on common carriers, landlords, or other specified persons. Now they can serve them on anyone and the order does not have to specify the name of the person required to assist.

Roving wiretap authority (the ability to tap various and multiple phones) raises serious Fourth Amendment problems because it relaxes the "particularity" requirements of the Warrant Clause, which means that a search must be very particular in the person and place to be searched. Such authority already exists under Title III. There is new authority that increases duration of FISA intercept orders. USAPA §207 amends 50 USC §1805(e) (1) concerning surveillance on agents of a foreign power (not U.S. persons) from 90 to 120 days.

- **FISA search warrants**

  Extend time for surveillance. USAPA §207 amends 50 USC §1824(d) for judicially authorized physical searches to a) **90 days** up from 45, or b) if the person is an agent of a foreign power (employee or member of a foreign power but not U.S. persons), **120 days**.

The Patriot Act Watching Your Money

The Intelligence Authorization Act of Fiscal Year 2004 was able to further expand the reach of the government through the Patriot Act. This attack on our civil liberties was launched on December 13, 2003 when President George W. Bush signed into law a bill giving the FBI new powers. I call this passage a secret because: 1). This bill was signed while Americans were celebrating the capture of Saddam Hussein; 2). The legislation was signed without any formal effective notice to the U.S. citizens; 3). Even worse is the fact that this legislation was buried inside a piece of legislation that would mask the average citizen's ability to realize its effect. Here are the details of the Intelligence Authorization Act of Fiscal Year 2004:

- The Act included a simple redefinition of "financial institution," which previously referred to banks, but now includes stockbrokers, car dealerships, casinos, credit card companies, insurance agencies, jewelers, airlines, the U.S. Post Office, and any other business whose cash transactions have a high degree of usefulness in criminal, tax or regulatory matters.

- To get financial information on any person from these types of businesses, the government need only make a request by way of a "National Security Letter." They don't have to appear before a judge for the normal probable cause hearing showing that the target is involved in criminal or terrorist activity.

- There is a gag order – the financial institution can not inform the target that his or her personal information is being shared, without that business being subject to a fine. In fact the target may never know, well until he is prosecuted.

Now that is the power of the Legal Matrix.

One of the worse parts of this new expansion of power is the fact that the FBI does not have to report to Congress how often they have used the National Security Letters. This prevents any type of oversight that can curtail abuses. We know from experience that oversight is important. Just look at the documentation of racial profiling in New Jersey which caused Congress to look into its occurrences. Without oversight how do we protect our liberty.

The Patriot Act In Action

As stated earlier, the fact that this legislation was placed deep within another piece of legislation shows that the Legal Matrix is in full effect. The Agent's intention was to keep the public from debating, and rejecting the plan. The Agents saw this reaction when the Bush administration attempted to pass what was nicknamed the Patriot Act II. The open debate caused the demise of that new act.

A September 27, 2003 news paper article by Eric Lichtblau reported that the Patriot Act has been used with increased frequency in many criminal investigations that have little or no connection to terrorism. The government has been using the expanded powers to investigate suspected drug traffickers, white-collar criminals, blackmailers, child pornographers, money launderers, spies, and even corrupt foreign leaders. They have been using the new powers in cases to investigate people, initiate wiretaps, and other surveillance. Now, I must admit that the expanded use of the Patriot Act has helped track and catch some criminals, but the question is whether we are giving up too much for too little.

> The financial institution can't inform the target that his or her personal information is being shared, without that business being subject to a fine. In fact the target may never know, well until he is prosecuted.

Underscoring changes in domestic surveillance allowed under the Patriot Act, the Justice Department said in a report released in May 2004, that it conducted hundreds more secret searches around the United States in 2003 under foreign intelligence surveillance laws. In an annual report to Congress, the Justice Department said that it obtained approval to conduct electronic surveillance and physical searches in more than 1,700 intelligence cases last year. In fact there were about 1,200 covert searches authorized in 2002. U.S. Attorney General John Ashcroft said, "These court-approved surveillance and search orders are vital to keeping America safe from terror."

At least 4 states and 270 communities officially have called for limitations to personal information, including library and medical records. A recent poll by the Nonpartisan Council for Excellence in Government found that most Americans, 56%, considered the Patriot Act a net plus for the country (Half also expressed concern about how the act is being applied).[xliii]

We have the choice to accept the Patriot Act or fight the Legal Matrix for change. Whatever you decide to do, knowledge is power, so we are now in a position to do something.

Program - The Ohio Concealed Weapon Law

Ohio has followed many other states in passing a concealed weapon law. Many people were excited about the law and considered it a valuable tool. However, like all the programs in the Legal Matrix, we know that the law is a tool but a tool for whom? Is it a tool to trap us in the system or a tool to protect us?

Is it a Tool to Protect Us?

Hopefully, the tone of this book does not sound totally negative. I want to be the first to endorse the sentiment that the Legal Matrix is about control, but the control can and often does benefit us. Many programs exist to protect us from harm, and to maintain order. Being robbed, assaulted or otherwise threatened are harms that we all want to avoid, so from that standpoint, the Legal Matrix does provide a benefit.

The Ohio concealed weapon law was passed in January 2004, allowing its residents to carry concealed weapons. The law on its face appears to provide us a tool for protection. So the thought process is that if we have a weapon or the ability to carry a weapon, then criminals will not act as fast to harm us.

There is another side of the story. The other side of the story again requires us to take the Red Pill and look deep into the likely effects of the new law. The ability to carry a concealed weapon can end up being another trap of the Legal Matrix. While I was in an interview of my client by a detective, the subject of this new law came up and one of the first reactions was that lawyers are going to make a lot of money. Why? Well the result will be more people getting charged with Carrying Weapons under Disability and many other fire arms charges. Even worse, these charges can be picked up by the Federal Government which will expose the person to the strict federal sentencing guidelines and to time in the hole of the Legal Matrix - Jail. So on the surface, this is a law to protect, but I am sure that you will have more people subject to criminal charges than those who will proclaim that their lives were saved because they carried a gun.

The Side Effect of the Concealed Weapon Law

One side effect of the concealed weapon law is that more police officers will be at risk. Police Officers - yes they are Agents but again, all Agents are not bad. There are the ones who help, and the ones who harm. Generally speaking the police officers are going to be the most affected group by this new law. Every person they approach on the street will potentially have a concealed weapon. This fact will cause the stress level of the job to rise to unbearable levels. Stress on the job may lead to stress at home, stress at home will cause officers to act out against the alleged criminals. Even worse, these Agents may end up getting caught in the Legal Matrix. I truly pray that the police officers will be able to handle the increased risk of this new law.

Some Laws, Although Well Intended, Simply Work Against Us

Example 1: The Federal Speedy Trial Act of 1974, as amended, 18 U.S.C. Section 1631, is an example of a protection

157

that we have that does not go far enough. The act requires that the trial for a criminal defendant be commenced within 70 days of the date of the indictment or (published) complaint; otherwise the alleged criminal is to be released. This is a necessary protection that many criminal defendants argued for. However, the application is less likely because most prosecutors are well aware of the time issue and, accordingly, they make sure that they get the case rolling, even if they have a very weak case. The flip side of this law is that once the defendant is convicted, there is no same urgency to determine whether the conviction was unlawful, when challenged. After a conviction, the wrongdoing is revealed to the court, usually, only when the incarcerated defendant files a habeas corpus petition or appeal, and that whole procedure can take about 3 years from date of conviction to date of release from prison (if the prisoner is successful), or about 1-2 years from the date of conviction if the prisoner is unsuccessful with his/her petition.

Example 2: On March 31, 2004, the U.S. Supreme Court ruled that border Agents have wide freedom to search vehicles entering the U.S., even if they do not have a specific reason to suspect wrongdoing. The Judge said that this ability serves the purpose to combat drug trafficking and terrorism. To combat the fact that more than 90 million Mexican vehicles enter the U.S. each year. This again is an example of the Legal Matrix strengthening its ability to control us through a law that appears to benefit us. What happens when the searches extend to places inside the United States, and then to people other than suspected Mexican smugglers?

Example 3: A ruling that we discussed earlier, and has caused me much dismay, is the case of *Maryland v. Pringle*.[xliv] In this case U.S. Supreme Court Held that being in a vehicle with friends or acquaintances, who are in possession of drugs or have them in the car, can put the unsuspecting innocent person in jail. "We think it an entirely reasonable inference that any or all three of the occupants had knowledge of and exercised dominion and control over the cocaine." The court was reiterating a holding in a similarly shocking case which ruled that "a car passenger – unlike the unwitting tavern patron - will often be engaged in a common enterprise with the driver and have the same interest in concealing the fruits or the evidence of their wrongdoing." This is a ruling and essentially a law that will have a lasting and devastating effect on the Legal Matrix and our lives for years to come.

So what do we do when the laws work against us? The only hope is that legislators like Representative John Conyers, D-Mich, will continue working to change the laws so that justice and fairness is extended to all Americans. We can also request the assistance of public people/celebrities like Russell Simmons, who has spent a large amount of time fighting the New York Rockefeller laws.

The Rockefeller laws, the first in the nation that require minimum sentences for first-time drug users, was enacted in 1973 in New York by then governor Nelson Rockefeller. It imposed harsh prison terms for the possession, or sale of relatively small amounts of drugs. The harshest provision of this statute mandates that a judge impose a prison term of no less than 15 years to life for anyone convicted of selling 2 ounces or possessing 4 ounces of a narcotic substance. The penalties apply without regard to the circumstances of the offense or the individual's character or background, making it irrelevant whether the person is a first-time or repeat offender. Currently, 93% of drug offenders in New York State Prisons are of African-American and Latino descent. Russell Simmons has been successful in getting his voice heard on this issue and making positive change.

Chapter IV
Living with the Legal Matrix without Falling for the Traps

Life in the Legal Matrix

It's been said that minorities in our society, minority by race, financial status, or power, yield because the majority has come into control of the police power of the state. Force is used due to the average person's inability to transcend his own interest to respect the interests of his fellow man. The force that guarantees peace can also bring injustice. Power is poison and it is a poison which blinds the eyes of moral insight and lames the will of moral purpose.

The Department of Justice issued a rule authorizing it to monitor communications between federal prison inmates and their counsel without court approval.

The government is supposed to exist at the will of the governed, and it is the plight of the governed that creates or should create the laws. That does not seem to be the case within the Legal Matrix. The man of power or dominant class which binds society together regulates it processes, always paying itself inordinate rewards for its labors.

Does knowledge lead to a just society? Yes. The sense of justice is a product of the mind, and not of the heart. It is the result of reason's insistence upon consistency. An irrational society accepts injustice because it does not analyze the pretensions made by the powerful and privileged groups of society. Men will not cease to be dishonest, merely because their dishonesties have been revealed or because they have discovered their own deception. Wherever men hold unequal power in society, they will strive to maintain it. They will use whatever means are most convenient to that end and will seek to justify them. So in order to ensure justice and endure life in the Legal Matrix, we must question, analyze, and then, when necessary, challenge the Legal Matrix.

Is it true that we define our existence as humans through pain? Whether we know it or not, we chose pain every day. Whenever we lack the wisdom to make sound choice, or we give in to selfish desires, we choose pain. In our attachment to temporal things, we chose pain. Even in our attachment to those we love we choose pain. Even when we don't' choose it seems to come upon us through the simple circumstances of life.[xlv]

Thomas Jefferson said "the art of life is the art of avoiding pain."

I had an experience with the Legal Matrix confirming that we must carefully watch the steps we take so that we can avoid the web. There was a new judge in the City of Cleveland, a woman whom I thought would be a great addition to the bench, but once I stood in front of her I was so shocked of her lackadaisical approach to the analysis of justice. In fact, her ruling caused the family that I was representing to call me four times an hour trying to get me to change her ruling. See in the Legal Matrix the family does not understand that the Neo's (the lawyers) only have so much power, the system is larger than any one of us and it is only through concerted effort that we can change the system. The judge had a chance to make a difference early in her career, by making an appropriate ruling in my case, but decided not to. She was only on the bench for about 3 months, but when judges take that position or more importantly when elected to that position, there is an expectation of service to the community that elected you. So to impress the community at large, that judge chose to administer pain through the use of the Legal Matrix.

My client had been accused of Aggravated Robbery of a police officer Felonious Assault and Resisting Arrest. Interestingly, these charges arose after he was beaten in front of his entire community. See Aggravated Robbery on a police officer is a statutory crime that includes any alleged attempt to grab an officer's gun. This is an accusation easy to make and when actually at trial, the presumption is that the officers do not lie. The charge that my client faced, attempting to take an officers gun, does not happen often. My client, a young college student with no record, was walking out of the home of a friend in his neighborhood. It is alleged that he was in possession of crack cocaine (that was never proven nor was he charged with such a crime), but this "probable cause" gave the officers the right to accost my client. Ultimately he was beaten and arrested. After time in the hospital, he spent 27 days in jail before getting his constitutional right to a preliminary hearing. It is the constitutional violations, of jailing him for 27 days without a preliminary hearing and the setting of a $50,000 cash only bond, which the Judge could have affected. The judge had the power to lower the bond, in fact she did. She later allowed the comments of a prosecutor, not interested in or sensitive to the rights of African Americans and highly focused on getting convictions, in objection to the lowered bond, she re-raised it. The prosecutor lied in open court and made allegations that were not part of any record, so the judge, against my adamant objections lowered the bond and then raised the bond again.

So what should the judge have done? Take the time, instead of rushing through her docket for whatever personal reason, and engage in an inquiry with the prosecutor, the defense attorney and the defendant about the facts of the case and allegations. Instead, my client was pushed through the system as another African American accused of a crime and presumed guilty.

Martha Stewart and Other Lessons of the Legal Matrix

Martha Stewart's illegal or questionable Imclone stock sales were worth $50,000, but her lost was about $400 million in legal cost, lost sales, and her freedom. That is the Legal Matrix. The system will love you to death and at the quickest blink; it will take you down and attack you.

Michael Tyler, better known as the Grammy-nominated **rapper Mystical,** 33 years old, was sentenced to six years in prison for forcing his hair stylist to perform sex acts. He plead guilty to sexual battery based on the victims accusation that he and two bodyguards forced her to perform oral sex after they accused her of stealing $80,000 worth of his checks. She denied stealing any money. The Legal Matrix took him when the evidence revealed he actually video taped the entire sexual episode.

In January 2004, a Chicago judge ordered R&B singer **R. Kelly** to have no contact with singer Michael Jackson at the 2004 Grammy awards. That is control to the highest extent, when the Legal Matrix tells us who we can communicate and associate with. Some call it probation and parole; I call it the Legal Matrix in full effect.

Speaking of probation, before his outstanding performance in the movie *Ray,* actor **Jamie Foxx** was on probation for a misdemeanor charge of disturbing the peace, stemming from a dispute with security guards at a New Orleans casino.

Even **Mike Tyson**, heavy weight champion of the world whose problems with the law and other people have been well and fully documented in the media, had the insight to comment on **Kobe Bryant's** problem stating that one moment you are on top of the world and everyone loves you, next you are in the system as a regular person. This is the whole purpose of the Legal Matrix to keep us all in check. To make sure that we all remember that we are regular people; all subject to the Legal Matrix.

Is the Legal Matrix Prejudice, Racially or Economically?

The question has been posed as to whether the Legal Matrix is a class or race based system. The system itself is color blind in most aspects. We are able to say that many times, African Americans and Hispanics may be the target group whom are affected by the system and its laws, but I submit that the system exists for everyone.

Instead of purely a racial inquiry, instead take an economical one. The question then becomes whether or not a person's status or financial ability affects the Legal Matrix's reach on that particular person. It does not, the system is the system. Like every system there are ways to trip it or break through. I refer to the ability to live outside the law of the Legal Matrix. The ability to exist on the fringes to get away with acts that others would be arrested for.

To further answer the prejudice question, in addition to targeting anyone who steps out of the boundaries of the Legal Matrix, I believe, and research supports the position, that the Legal Matrix targets specific people and their actions. If you make too much money, create too much value or get too high on your horse, the Legal Matrix will take you down. Take for instance the federal indictments handed down in a governmental corruption case that charged many elected officials and a business man in Cleveland, Ohio. One well respected journalist in Cleveland, Sam Fulwood III made the observation that federal prosecutors failed to indict the big corporations that were the source of the monetary funds that were allegedly used in the corruption of public officials. The case stems from the investigation and conviction of a city mayor for taking bribes from a Cleveland businessman Nate Gray in an effort to position Mr. Gray's associates, many big corporations, in better position to get government contracts. The bottom line is that the Legal Matrix went after Nate Gray, an African American businessman, instead of going after the companies who benefited from the alleged bribes. The fact of the matter is that Nate Gray's actions were funded by the big corporations which defended themselves by claiming that they were unaware of his actions on the corporation's behalf. The Legal Matrix let that reasoning fly and did not indict the corporate officials.

In November 2003, a Cleveland, Ohio community activist was arraigned on allegations of rape and sexual imposition in an incident that occurred 15 years prior. The interesting thing is that, his involvement in the system came on the back end of his involvement in a search for a young girl in Cleveland who was kidnapped, brutally killed and found in a field. It was during the search for this young girl that television reporters gathered the information that caused him to become subject to these allegations. His alleged victim and her mother both recanted the young lady's former statement but that did not protect him from the Legal Matrix. His bond was set at $250,000.

William Green - Cleveland Browns running back - was drafted with the high expectations of helping to bring excitement back to the team and the city of Cleveland. Although he had all the potential in the world, he became subject to the Legal Matrix in a few situations. First, he was required to adhere to the NFL substance monitoring, due to the discovery of and his acknowledgment of a substance abuse problem. Secondly, the Legal Matrix absorbed him once he was found to have marijuana on his person. Third, when his personal life became public an incident of domestic violence, where he was the victim, gave him additional unwanted notice and exposure to the Legal Matrix.

Although his girlfriend was the suspect of this violence, the police executed a search warrant on the running back's home. Remember, he was not charged with a crime, it was his girlfriend who was a suspect, yet police officers searched the home, took items such as cigarette butts, tennis shoes and other personal items that belonged to the NFL running back. At that time the officers were looking for illegal substances, not anything to support the Domestic Violence charge. It is another example of how the Legal Matrix will catch you.

Rush Limbaugh in the Legal Matrix – such an irony. He spent much of his time speaking against criminals and specifically drug users and dealers yet; the Legal Matrix uncovered his addiction to prescription medication. He is accused of doctor shopping to obtain the drugs, and has now fought very hard to get the system off his back.

As the Legal Matrix advances we are forced to deal with the society at large who through the acknowledgement of fears, accepts, and even encourages the Legal Matrix's growth. The evidence of society's desire to keep the Legal Matrix growing is the support for increased enforcement of laws. For instance, in 2004, when two NBA teams, the Indiana Pacers and the Detroit Pistons got into a "brawl" in Detroit, there were people and pundits who expressed the desire for fans and the athletes to be criminally prosecuted. I understand that they want **Order** out of the **Chaos** but I was amazed at the fact that there was a push for legal and penal involvement. This happens everyday. When there is a problem people run to the authorities, and request its involvement. This cry for help is then enforced by politicians and lawmakers. The way that John Ashcroft trampled on our civil liberties is an example of the desire to gain power through the Legal Matrix, and again, there were those who fully supported the laws that he enacted.

The Matrix can be compared to a spider web. It is always growing, covering more area and getting tighter. This is how the Legal Matrix works. The laws are expanding into more areas that were protected by the Bill of Rights while more everyday activities are being scrutinized and criminalized.

"The greatest menace to freedom is an inert people." Justice Louis Brandeis

The Legal Matrix Can Create Bad Alliances

There were many times, while in court defending my clients, where I sensed a weird connection between the presiding judge and the prosecuting attorney – two Agents of the system. It almost felt as if my clients could not get a fair shake, and too many of the people with power were pushing for a settlement that would put my clients in the grasp of the Legal Matrix, in jail. There have been situations where, without a blink, the prosecutor and the judge both offered to give my client a "deal" of one year in prison. It is amazing to me that taking away a year of another person's life is not really considered the tragedy that it is. For those who have never been to prison, there is nothing easy or acceptable about "taking" a year.

In one situation I had a client who was charged with Felonious Assault as a result of an adulterous relationship between my client's husband and his girlfriend. The event occurred when my client went looking for her husband at the mistress' home. The mistress came out and began to physically and verbally beat up my client. My client ended up with scratches and bruises. However, as my client was attempting to leave the scene, the mistress, now turned victim, ran into the street and was hit by my client. Of course, my client did not feel she was in the wrong and most importantly, my client did not form the intent to harm the victim. I was told it was an accident. My client could not understand why she should plead and agree to "take" a year when she did not do anything intentionally.

This story has two points of interest. First, it shows just how easily our everyday life activities can lead us, if we are not careful, into the Legal Matrix. Second, the Legal Matrix is stacked against us all. The system itself is created to control, and once you are caught in it the goal is to control you. "Taking" a year does not seem to be a big deal for the system designed to do just that "take."

Surveillance in the Legal Matrix

As time goes on and technology increases the Legal Matrix becomes stronger and stronger. For instance, the surveillance abilities and actual practices in this country are indicators of the Legal Matrix at work. In Washington D.C there are over 700 cameras in operation that watch over the citizen's everyday moves while they maneuver the public streets of D.C. This practice has increased all over the country. Even in Cleveland, Ohio, in the Collinwood area, there are surveillance cameras that constantly monitor and tape the main streets. The problem is that there is a strain between our **Fourth Amendment** rights against unreasonable searches and seizures and the public's desire and need to feel and actually be protected. There are some cities that use high powered interconnected and intelligent cameras that are linked to databases. There are strong accusations that these surveillances have been used to profile and harass certain individuals.

The very nature of the Legal Matrix is to gain greater control over our lives. Remember that it was created to control chaos, and now that we have embraced the need to control chaos at all costs, the Legal Matrix is growing. As author Christian Parenti noted in his book - *Surveillance in America*[xlvi], the net is widening and the mesh is thinning. Meaning the net of police power is widening to cover more types of allegedly deviant behaviors and at the same time deviance is defined down to include ever more small activities and behavior being criminalized. Take for instance some of the things that schools have criminalized and used cameras to enforce - bad behavior on buses, skateboarding, and displays of affection in school. Although many people in this country support having such acts criminalized, we must be careful that we protect the rights of others so that our rights may be intact.

The attempt to control our society has a long history in this country. Take for instance the late 1910s and early 1920s when J Edgar Hoover and his cronies launched massive attacks on Americans whom were considered a danger to the society at large, or more importantly the government itself.

Today, control is being established over our society in the most intruding ways. Through the use of credit cards, ATM cards, electronic tolls, cell phones and other electronics we are leaving footprints behind to show where we are or where we have been. We our voluntarily adding to the systems control by our use of these devises.

A Law Enforcement Technology survey found that 41% of local police departments and 66% of state police departments used fixed site video surveillance cameras.[xlvii]

One Felony, No Vote?

A survey of our country indicates that 48 states have some type of restriction on the voting rights of convicted felons. My friend, this is not a small situation. Although we all were given the right to vote by the constitution and Bill of Rights, the Legal Matrix found a way to affect that right. When you look at the fact that on any given day approximately one African-American man out of three, between the ages of 20 and 29 is behind bars or on probation or parole, we see that the felon voting restrictions is a problem. So in the context of a trap, it is undeniable that by catching a felony you jeopardize your ability to be successful in the Legal Matrix and to affect change of the Legal Matrix by placing your vote. Luckily, many States allow you to vote after the periods of parole or probation. Why even risk it?

Your focus is your reality. If you focus on the negative, you will live and receive the negative.

You Never Know a Person Until You Fight Them.

There was a scene in *The Matrix Reloaded* where Neo wanted to see the Oracle, (the person with "all knowledge"), but was approached by her protector. The protector would not let Neo pass without first challenging him to a fight. The lesson from this scene is that you will never know the true essence of a person or laws until you are forced to confront the situation. Take for example **divorce**. You never know the pain of divorce until you are in the middle of it. People talk about the statistics all the time, they talk about the destruction that divorce causes to a family and the financial ruins that the situation can leave you in. You won't know the disaster until you confront the situation for yourself. If the opposite where true, and we where aware of the essence of the situation the divorce rate would not be that high. We would think seriously about the relationships that we get in, so that divorce would be less likely, or we would work harder to prevent it from happening (Nonetheless, we know that divorce occurs because we do not know the true essence of the situation until you fight it for yourself).

> You never know the pain of divorce until you are in the middle of it.

The same can be said for just about any area of the Legal Matrix, you must fight the fight to truly know the person or situation. The purpose of this book is to keep you from having to know the situation for yourself. By providing you with the proper education and understanding of the Legal Matrix you can avoid the circumstances that burden and bond so many people.

The Legal Matrix is strict and we must know the system in order to survive with it. At the end of the Matrix trilogy, Neo came in direct contact with the construct of the Matrix and they finally reach harmony. That's how we must live our individual lives, we must get in touch with the Matrix through knowledge and understanding and then we can live in harmony with the system.

The first thing that we must remember about the Legal Matrix is that we are a number; the system does not care about you or me. When you catch a case and end up in the system, you become an expected statistic. You are expected to slip up, expected to lose your temper and get in to a fight (facing the possibility of an assault charge), expected to run a red light (facing points on your license and a fine), expected to make bad relationship decisions (facing the possibility of civil or criminal charges).

> You will not truly understand it until you are caught in the system

I submit that we must avoid the traps of the Legal Matrix at all costs. No one can be told what the Legal Matrix is; you must see it for yourself. This is the sad reality. This text will give you the information, and knowledge to help. Nevertheless, you will never truly know the Legal Matrix until you see it for yourself. The examples of people who suddenly found themselves subject to the Legal Matrix show that the system can take you off guard and by surprise. Just look at the circumstances of Rush Limbaugh and Maurice Clarret.

Maurice Clarret was a star running back for the National Champion Ohio State Buckeye football team. During his freshman year at the school he was loved, admired, and gained national status as an all American running back. He did not realize that he was also subject to the Legal Matrix. He did not know the tools necessary to remain in his position of glory. The very next season, he took a misstep that caused the Legal Matrix to become visible in his life. He experienced, vilification, disgrace, and removal from the Ohio State team, all in one year. He was a freshman sitting on top of the world, planning his eventual entry into the NFL. However, after his record breaking season, the Legal Matrix fell upon him. He was under investigation for making a false police report concerning a stolen vehicle. He was questioned about having the vehicle and the dollar value of its contents. He was even investigated concerning his attendance and classroom performance. Eventually these situations caused him to be suspended from the team, led to a failed bid to enter the NFL, and he was unable to play for the entire next season. The Ohio State Buckeyes fell short of the glory that they had in the 2002-2003 season.

> I don't want to infer that the Legal Matrix is designed to cause us to fail or is a system created to make our lives full of suffering or pain, but the system is designed to keep us in line with the laws that are in existence.

These are examples of the fact that no matter how much you hear about the Legal Matrix, you will not truly understand it until you are caught in the system.

I don't want to infer that the Legal Matrix is designed to cause us to fail or is a system created to make our lives full of suffering or pain. The system is designed to keep us in line with the laws that are in existence. The good thing about the Legal Matrix is that the programs can be tampered with. Remember rules can be bent and others broken. This means that the laws can change, whether by grass roots efforts, elections, or courtroom battles. We can change the law that effect us but we can not get rid of the matrix.

We control our existence in the Legal Matrix. We are in control of our destiny. That's a short coming of the Legal Matrix. The Legal Matrix cannot control our free will, our motivation, or our minds. Life here on earth, unlike *The Matrix* movie, does not have a cosmic force controlling our minds. Although much research has been dedicated to the theory, it has not been proven that we are mentally controlled by a greater power. Even most hard core religious zealots confirm that we exist under the arm of free will. That being said, the Legal Matrix can be bent based on our desires and our will.

> The problem is that people will do whatever they deem is necessary to survive, so if that means people must drive illegally to provide food on the table or care for a loved one, they will.

We can live in the Legal Matrix without being noticed by the system itself. As soon as we venture outside the system and live outside the norms we will be subject to the Legal Matrix's close scrutiny and then possibly the system itself. That is what the Legal Matrix will do to you, that's what it's designed to do - utilize the legal system to keep us all in check.

One of the problems in American society, and society at large, is the lack of knowledge. People get into trouble because they don't understand the system. For instance, in Ohio there are new laws dealing with Driving While Intoxicated, Vehicle Insurance, and an array of other driving issues. If you are caught breaking various laws in Ohio, you may end up without driving privileges. See privilege means that there is no absolute right to drive, but we are allowed to do so at the state's allowance. If the state takes away your license, what will the result be? How will you get to work? How will you care for your child? The problem is that people will do whatever they deem is necessary to survive, so if that means people must drive illegally to provide food on the table or care for a loved one, they will. Inevitably there will be charges for driving without a license. There will be charges for fraud, falsification and many other related charges. The circle of destruction will continue to exist.

The Legal Matrix is the "Terminator (times) 3"

There is a great action thriller that starred the now governor of California Arnold Swartzeneger – *Terminator 3*. The movie is based on the premise that the United States, in all its glory, created a computer system that ultimately took on a mind of its own and destroyed the world. Basically, we created the system that in turn destroyed mankind. The same can be associated with the Legal Matrix. The government created a legal system that, if left unchecked by citizens and activists, may one day destroy the freedom and liberties that we enjoy as Americans. The problem with *The Terminator* movie was that once the system became self sustaining it could not be stopped. If we continue to chip away at the core of the Constitution and Bill of Rights, there will be no end to the erosion of our liberties.

The Legal Matrix as a "Minority Report"

In the movie, *Minority Report*, Tom Cruise, played a dynamic role as a chief investigator in the fictional pre-crime division of the futuristic Washington D.C. police force. This division was created to fight the increasingly rising murder rate by identifying, and stopping crimes before they actually take place.

The system worked on the ability to predict, within hours, murders that were about to occur so that the police force could prevent its occurrence. At one point in the movie, there is a federal agent who poses a question of the constitutionality of arresting people for crimes that they did not commit, but were about to commit. The answer was that the system had a 100% guarantee of accuracy. In the opinions of the creator and the officers, the machine could never be wrong.

The relevance of the movie to our study is the fact that, if left unchecked, the Legal Matrix, though it may not physically destroy us as in the *Terminator 3*, will put further clamps on our existence. It's like a ceiling. The ceiling will get lower and lower until our freedom does not exist. Like *Minority Report* the Legal Matrix will eventually be able to crush us for our plans, perceived intentions and thoughts. Some would say that we are already under attack for our thoughts, at least when we express them out loud. Oh, but I forgot we are supposed to have the protections of the First Amendment. Present history shows that there is a battle over what can and cannot be protected by free speech. Look at a recent example with the multi-platinum, millionaire rapper Eminem. He was recently under a brief investigation for lyrics that he put in one of his rap songs. The lyrics talked about his desire for "dead presidents." However, before getting all uptight about the lyrics, it would have saved the government some time, money, and effort if they would have recognized that "dead presidents" is slang expression for money. Even earlier in rap history the 2 live Crew was put under national spotlight for some of the lyrics they expressed. Maybe the depiction in *Minority Report* is not so far fetched. The government is doing many things to win the war against terrorism and you never know how far they will go.

Freedom–Avoid The Traps of the System

The Legal Matrix Will Attempt to Link You to That Which Will Bring You Under Its Control.

Is the mystery of the Legal Matrix solved by knowing that the Agents and Programs are attempting to control our lives? That they exist to keep us from chaos and there is nothing that we can do about it? My answer is no. With knowledge comes power. Knowing the Legal Matrix and understanding it gives us the ability and the power to exist within the Legal Matrix and to be successful. As we discovered earlier, although the Legal Matrix has control, we also have control. We control our mind, actions, and our emotions. The good part about our control is that if it is properly exerted, we lessen the possibility of being a victim to the Legal Matrix.

The traps are endless so in this first edition I will discuss a few.

1. Emotionalism

All humans have emotions and we all react to situations in different manners. Because emotions are a natural part of our existence, there is no problem with having emotions. As we all know, emotions can be a positive thing. They help us react when we are in danger. They give us the ability to reach out to others. However, our emotions are not monitored or controlled by our mind and they are allowed to dictate our actions, we are likely to fall into the trap of the Legal Matrix and destruction.

In order to properly deal with our emotions, we must recognize that our emotions are the product of feelings. Feelings are the product of perceptions. It is our perception of situations that gives us feelings and then causes our emotions to react. Here are two examples:

> We must force ourselves to be patient and wait to learn the true facts of a situation before we react and either damage ourselves or a relationship.

- You see your mate walking down the street with a beautiful person of the opposite sex. You believe or **perceive** that your mate is being unfaithful. You begin to **feel** jealous. Then you are lead, by your emotions, to go and start a confrontation.

   ** *The real situation is that the person was a co-worker and the mate was not cheating.*

- You are stopped by a police officer for a traffic violation. You are disturbed because you believe or **perceive** that you did not commit a moving violation. You **feel** that you are being targeted. You tell the officer just how you feel.

   ** *The real situation is that you were being stopped for a bad taillight that you did not know was out. The taillight helps keep you safe.*

In both of the above examples, emotions where allowed to guide the person's actions. Each person was momentarily out of control based on emotionalism.

The laws of the Legal Matrix are not about perception but instead they are about hard core facts. At least that's what the design is supposed to be. That being the case, obviously we should not make decisions based on feelings, or perceptions when we know that fact exists. We must force ourselves to be patient and wait to learn the true facts of a situation before we react and either damage ourselves or a relationship. Example:

> **Emotion:** allowing our emotions to cause an assault on a spouse or family member based on a feeling or perception

> **Fact:** Domestic violence will lead to incarceration.

You have to control your emotions. Emotions are like hungry children, they are always ready to feed. If your emotions are not balanced with knowledge and control, they will mislead you.

"So much emotion over something so small - it's just a kiss."

There was a scene in the second Matrix movie where Neo and his team were given the opportunity to get closer to solving the mystery of the Matrix and thereby save Zion. During this scene a beautiful woman tells the crew that she will take them to the key maker in exchange for a kiss from Neo. Specifically she wanted a kiss that was full of passion and expression. Neo's girlfriend, Trinity, did not want to allow the two to kiss and expressed her jealousy. The woman expressed amazement over the fact that there was so much jealousy and emotion over such a little thing as a kiss. That my friend is the truth of the matter.

We tend to show so much emotion over the little things. The inability to put emotion aside and deal with the issues and situations is what causes much of our destruction. An inventory of case logs and dockets across the nation will show that bad decisions, ones that are often tied to emotional decisions are the cause of many of our run-ins with the Legal Matrix. During my service as public defender, (A program in the Legal Matrix, not an Agent, designed to assist), there was a client accused of breaking and entering, kidnapping, and assault with a gun, all based on the failure to separate emotion from the situation. The client, a 19 year old lady, was in a relationship where she had a child with a guy. This was her third child, and the other children had different fathers. The relationship turned bad and at some point, the guy decided that he no longer wanted to be with the client and that he and his new girlfriend would raise the newborn child. At some point, the defendant agreed with this arrangement. As expected, things changed, she wanted her newborn back and felt threatened by the relationship that the new girlfriend had with the old boyfriend and the newborn. Instead of thinking outside the cloud of emotion, the client decided to take matters into her own hands. After numerous disputes, one evening she went to the new girlfriend's home, the defendant let herself in, pulled out a weapon (I still contest the allegation that it was a gun, my client says it was a knife), made the girlfriend leave the house, with the girlfriend's two year old child (child endangerment) made them get into her car and then drove them away. Somehow this event ended without either party being fatally injured, but the criminal charges came and this 19 year old girl's first experience with the Legal Matrix began.

So much emotion over such a little thing (losing your boyfriend, husband, wife, or mate to another person) that causes so much chaos. Instead of looking directly at the situation with out the cloud of emotion, we find ourselves in a desperate frame of mind. A close look at the situation will reveal that if the person has decided to leave you for another person, they have made up their mind not to be with you at this time. There is essentially nothing that you can do to prohibit the person from pursuing the other relationship. The only solution, the non-emotional solution, is to remove yourself from the equation - walk away. If the person comes back to you, then make your decision at that time. Do not expose yourself to embarrassment, disappointment and most importantly the consequences of the Legal Matrix.

2. Failure to just Get Along with Each Other – Domestic Relations

One of the most deceiving areas of the legal Matrix is the domestic relations end. It is in domestic relations court where the parties put themselves inside the Legal Matrix. The system does not usually knock on your door and ask if there are problems in your home. We invite the system in. The failure of individuals to communicate, and resolve their issues are the problem. Most of the cases in Domestic Relations court stem from two people refusing to communicate, or at least to look at the situation in a spirit of resolution as oppose to looking at it in a spirit of conflict.

Let's take a look at divorce. Today it should be obvious that divorce is a lose / lose situation. There was a desire, a dream, a plan, and they all failed. Of course emotions are high and people are disappointed. That does not mean that resolution can not be obtained. A major problem in most divorce cases is that one of the parties does not want the relationship to end. They feel that they are being wronged, or forced into the situation. That feeling alone causes conflict; add, on top of that, all property and the children. Instead of thinking about the divorce realistically, the parties are upset and trying to salvage more than the other person. Trying to hurt each other.

I have handled cases where the mother purposely attempts to keep the father from seeing his children. Instead of the parties working together for the benefit of the child, all of a sudden you hear more terms like, my children, as if they are exclusive to one parent. Most level-headed people realize that it is in the child's best interest to have a relationship with both parents. Even if one of the parents is not as desirable as the other wishes he/she to be, the child has a right to have a relationship with both parents. Regardless of how the parties feel about each other or how they want to dominate the child's life, the Court is charged to make decisions that take into account the child's best interests, not the parents. After thousands of dollars in attorney fees and countless hours in negotiation, it is the child, not either parent, who wins.

Divorcées often lose sight of this fact while in the heat of the battle. The same is true for visitation situations. It should be unnecessary for a father to be forced to file for court ordered visitation in order to see his children. But everyday in every town, there are situations where fathers are not allowed to visit there children. In the end, who gets the blame? The attorneys. Domestic relations is a thankless part of the law, but it is as necessary as the air we breathe. Until we are able to use an open mind and put emotionalism behind us, we will need the Legal Matrix to further dominate our lives by forcing us to act and dictating how we handle our family matters.

I often receive late night calls from clients who are overwhelmed by their relationships and in despair over the treatment they have received from the person who they had a child with, or in common slang the "Baby's mama or daddy." These calls often lead me to the first conclusion, and it goes back to a common theme of navigating the Legal Matrix, we have to be careful and mindful of the choices that we make. Why did this person chose that mate? The answer often lies in our old friend emotionalism. Making decisions based on the prevailing emotion. It takes discipline and a strong sense of purpose not to get caught in the trap of having children out of wedlock, having children much too young or having children with a person who you know does not have the best parenting qualities. The calls that I often field for my clients are just a need to vent and to receive some comfort. Even though many of the calls entail some type of demand on the attorney or an expression of disappointment, in the end the client knows, or should give some thought to the fact, that he or she made a very bad decision that they will have to live with. They will be forced to live with the person they chose to have a child with.

3. Ignorance

"We can never see past the choices that we don't understand." This was a line in the Matrix series that has real world application. The statement is as profound as it is hard to explain. Nevertheless the importance of this statement to the Legal Matrix is undeniable. Everyday people are getting caught in the Legal Matrix. The reason, beyond the mistakes, emotionalism and dumb decisions, is that they do not understand. They are ignorant to the system itself; ignorant of the Legal Matrix. Many people do not understand the gravity of decisions; do not understand the lasting effect of the things we choose to do. If we understood the Legal Matrix as well as we should, less people would be in courts and in jail.

A simple example could be the fact that before I became an attorney, I had several license suspensions, but since starting my own practice, I have not gotten a ticket. Why? The answer is that I now understand the workings and motives of the system, the Legal Matrix. Before I became a lawyer, I never thought it was wrong to get "hooked up" at a store (someone giving a person an unauthorized discount, or some other form of discount). Now, as an attorney, I understand how easy it would be to get charged with receiving stolen property.

By being knowledgeable about the Legal Matrix, we will be able to make the choices that will keep us out of the Legal Matrix so that we can make a choice to remain out of it. It's all about choices and understanding.

- If we understood the Legal Matrix, we wouldn't decide to sell drugs as an occupation. We would know that being in the industry exposes us to being a victim of schemes, attacks, deadly situations and the possibility of jail.

- If we understood the Legal Matrix, we wouldn't have children out of wedlock. We would know child support, custody and other issues will cause you endless days and nights of stress.

- If we understood the Legal Matrix, we wouldn't allow ourselves to have associations that are detrimental to our future. We would know that the Legal Matrix will entangle you in situations even if you have done nothing illegal.

- If we understood the Legal Matrix, we wouldn't decide to break the law by committing robberies, theft, or other crimes against property. Understanding would help us see that this type of activity will create bad karma so that your property may be invaded, you may injured by your target or end in jail.

- If we understood the Legal Matrix, we would not decide to commit assaults, domestic violence, battery or other crimes against the person. Understanding would help us see that we will get the same treatment that we give to others and the criminal laws will cause you to be put in jail.

The key is to seek understanding and knowledge. I tell the audience of my weekly radio show, we must educate ourselves continuously. The world is constantly changing so we must change with it. The Legal Matrix is improving and getting stronger. We must seek to understand it so that we can see and correctly make choices.

We can't see past the choices that we don't understand.

- We won't be able to see why America went to war with Iraq in the 90's if we don't understand the issues.

- We can't see why America went to war with Iraq in 2003 if we don't understand the issues.

- We can't see why the Department of Justice is attempting to take away our civil liberties if we do not understand history, the present, and the issues that appear to be most important to them now.

- We can't see past our mate leaving us, if we can not understand what they went through.

- We can't see past the fact that someone disrespected us if we can not understand what the other person is thinking, or is going through mentally. If we take the time to consider the other person's thoughts, or failure to think, we would decrease the accounts of road rage, assaults, arguments, and disputes.

The message is we must attempt to understand. The best way to do this is to remove yourself from the situation, even if only temporarily, and take time to think.

With Knowledge Comes Power

Why is it that when the oppressed are freed, they often begin to oppress others? We often enslave ourselves. Even the ordeal of our own personal freedom can become a form of slavery. No group of humans is immune from the desire to oppress. Even the goal to gain control of others becomes the master to which we are enslaved. We can become enslaved to our on selfish desires.

The first thing that starts to happen when we gain some type of advantage over other people is to treat others in a disrespectful manner. We must do all that we can to maintain our connection with the struggle. With the knowledge of the Legal Matrix and the ability to work for the Legal Matrix, we must make sure that we utilize these positions to promote the general good of all man kind. I know that particular statement sounds very "dreamy," but it is the truth.

The challenge goes like this. The people who are poor and on a "lower" socioeconomic standing in life or within the Legal Matrix have the challenge of remaining spiritual and in touch with the laws of the universe. They will be tempted to do whatever it takes to "survive," even if it means breaking the rules of the Legal Matrix. On the other hand, those people who are in power or in positions of comfort, such that they never worry about where the next meal is coming from or if the mortgage or rent will be paid in a particular month, have the challenge of being compassionate, understanding, and willing to help those who are less fortunate. It's been said that a rich man has difficulty getting into heaven. I submit that one of the reasons for this is that the willingness to do helpful deeds, without being judgmental is non-existence (There are exceptions and we will discuss them later).

The mind is its own place. It can make a hell out of heaven or heaven out of hell. As long as we don't allow our knowledge to blind us, and seek understanding of the Legal Matrix, we will be okay.

4. Living Outside the Law

In spite of the Legal Matrix and the traps that exist, some rules can be bent and others broken without consequence. Many people are able to successfully live outside the law of the Legal Matrix. Traditionally, athletes and entertainers, with their high paying salaries and lavish lifestyles, have been the exception to the rules of the Legal Matrix. These individuals are able to live beyond the means of most average people. They have the benefit of getting perks, compliments, and all types of accommodations. They are even prosecuted less than others. When or if they are prosecuted they can afford to "shake" the Legal Matrix with the best influence and attorneys that money can buy.

However, the Legal Matrix is the system under which we all live, so there is no one who can avoid the Legal Matrix and consistently live outside law. If we take a look at the Kobe Bryant situation, we see a person who had the privilege of living outside the law. He lives a lifestyle that many Americans dream of. Astonishing athletic ability, a diverse background having lived abroad, supportive and successful parents, celebrity and more money than most people imagine having. Yet, he fell victim to the Legal Matrix.

I have a colleague who stayed with the theory that we can live outside the law. That we can be successful in the world without playing and acknowledging that the Legal Matrix exists. I beg to differ, there is no way to consistently live outside the law and be successful. Drug dealers live outside the law, thieves live outside the law. These criminals, as well as all others always get caught.

5. The Illusion of Control

The illusion that many of us have is, that we control the world in which we live. That is the illusion that we all create in our own minds. For too long we have been existing without acknowledging that the system controls our everyday moves.

Under this illusion of control, there is the element that we must be involved in order to facilitate some type of change. The system is heartless and the laws that exist are for all people. It is the application of these laws, and the modification of the laws that we can change. Don't allow yourself to be disconnected from the system. Don't allow the feeling of disenfranchisement to keep you from being active to change the Legal Matrix. The "Vote or Die" campaign of Sean P Diddy Combs spoke directly to this position.

Another part of the illusion is the belief that you can sit back and not participate in the system and have some type of control over you life – it is impossible. The only way to remotely help yourself is to exist within the Legal Matrix, learn the workings of the Legal Matrix, vote, and try to affect the Legal Matrix.

50 cent, hip hop artist and pop icon, made many profound statements in his written work. One such comment was that "no

one grows up planning to sell drugs." I can take this a step further; no one grows up planning to go to jail, but the Legal Matrix is designed so that you may end up with this result. 50 cent also said "I don't say only God can judge me because I see things clear..." The Legal Matrix has the ability to judge you through laws, enactments, and judges and it does so everyday in every city and state across the nation. Speaking of the rap artist 50 cent, there is another illusion that is prevalent in our everyday lives and that affect us within the Legal Matrix. This illusion is that the words rappers speak are all true and reality. That couldn't be further from the truth. Most rappers will admit that, although their music is based on real life experiences and exposure, the music is just entertainment. For instance, Jay Z has not "removed a roof" (shot anyone with a gun), Eminem did not kill the mother of his child, the list goes on.

The Legal Matrix is the system that we are a part of and it encompasses all parts of our lives. Once you are aware of the Legal Matrix you can live life to the fullest and enjoy all of its varied fruits. Take for example "gansta rap," truth be told, there are only a few hundred or more artists who have become rich from making records. Others may have accomplished a nice lifestyle, but not every person on the radio is rich. On the other side, there are thousands of people whose lives are affected by the music that they hear. People who think the pimp mentality is reality for them. People who get involved in the war of words between rappers as evidenced once in our historic rap war of coasts. That is a prime example of the Legal Matrix. Those lifestyles are not normal, not a reality. Instead it is a screen that displays images in front of us, images that are not real and will eventually lead us to jail. If we are knowledgeable about the Legal Matrix, then we can hear the music, enjoy the music but realize that it is not a reality but a form of entertainment; an illusion. If we cannot come to grip with this fact, the music and interaction with it will put you in the Legal Matrix.

Help is on the Way!
Freedom - The Oracle:

Keeping with the Matrix theme, an Oracle represents wisdom and knowledge. In *The Matrix* movie, the Oracle was the program/person who helped unravel the mysteries of the Matrix. The Oracle was depicted by an old wise woman who had the answers before the questions were even posed. In our life, the Oracle helps us understand. In *The Matrix* movie sequels its discovered that the Oracle was not a person "free" from the Matrix, instead, she was a program that was created to keep balance. So what is balance?

The balance is between good and evil, the balance is between our desires versus the desires of the system to control us. The Oracle's purpose was to provide the necessary information so that the fight could continue. In ancient mythical times the Oracle was the wisest in the land. Going to the Oracle guaranteed the most accurate and helpful information. Today, the Oracle represents the information and resources that we have to help us in the Legal Matrix.

The Oracles may not look as we expect them to look so we must be willing to accept them as they come and work with them, not against them. If you don't know any Oracles, look a little closer and you will see people working very hard behind the scenes to keep the balance in this system. This text is an example of the Oracles at work. It will give you the information necessary to succeed in the Legal Matrix.

The form of instruction may be to encourage or just to provide examples. The form of instructions or life lessons may come from strangers, people whom we know or even educational materials. Through my practice and from my experiences, I have dedicated a large part of my life to helping people maximize their potential. I have experienced life's highs and lows. I am overwhelmed with passion when I am challenged concerning my understanding of the drug industry, specifically, my understanding of the mentality of the young men and women who risk their lives and freedom by choosing to participate in the illegal drug trade.

Oracles come in all shapes and sizes. They are a source of informed inspiration. Often times we are unaware why a specific person or challenge was placed in our lives. Then we realize that it gave us better understanding and strength. That is the purpose of an Oracle.

Defense Attorneys as an Oracle

At the end of the day, the defense attorney is the key to navigating the Legal Matrix, but sometimes, the defense attorney also fails. Sometimes the defense attorneys are prevented from effecting change by the very nature of the corrupt system.

> Defense attorneys and prosecutors work together on many cases and if a defense attorney pushes too hard, he will create a bad relationship with the prosecutor's office.

The first obvious problem is the reality that defense attorneys and prosecutors work together on many cases. If a defense attorney pushes too hard, he can create a bad relationship with the prosecutor's office. This bad blood will result in prosecutors not offering "good" plea agreements, and defense attorneys being forced to try more cases. At first glance having more trials does not sound like a bad ideal, but on a practical level it would not work. Time is money, and if all an attorney's time is spent in trial, that attorney would likely end up bankrupt. Understand that attorneys are use to taking large sums of money from most of their clients without having to defend the client at trial. Statistically, more than 95% of the federal convictions are based on guilty pleas, so that means only 1 case out of 20 convictions is a result of an actual trial. If a criminal lawyer trying to challenge the system had to try 20 times as many cases, he/she would not have the time to try the cases along with the other responsibilities of life, and would lose substantial revenues by being unable to take any more cases. Good attorneys are not concerned about the money; instead they are concerned about justice. There are good defense attorneys out there.

Indigent Defendants Lost in the Legal Matrix

The next situation is that the government is not putting forth the necessary financial resources toward defending indigent persons. Lawyers representing *The New York Times* and IBM receive about $500 per hour for their work in a federal action. often with 3 to 4 lawyers working on the same matter at the same time together with other support personnel. Lawyers representing indigent criminal defendants in a federal criminal action are paid about $35 per hour, which is obviously and deliberately insufficient to obtain competent representation.

> For the record, every attorney has the same training and ability – even public defenders.

If it costs $30,000 per year to maintain a prisoner, (including an allocation for the cost of the building the prison cell itself, and shared facilities), at least $150 per hour in legal fees for attorneys defending indigent defendants would probably result in far less of an expense to have a defendant found innocent than the cost of imprisonment if convicted, at least when the sentence is, say, 5 years or more. We could actually reduce the prison population by 70% to 90% over a 20-year period, and more than pay for the higher legal fees. The truth of the matter is that the legal system is failing indigent defendants. These particular defendants often feel that the attorney is not a "real" attorney, which is a ridiculous assertion. For the record, every attorney has the same training and knowledge – even public defenders. The only difference between a public defender and a private attorney is that the private attorney is paid more to defend a person's interests, whereas the public defender is paid far less and expected to give the same attention – that does not always happen.

Freedom - The Neo's

The people who go to great lengths and often potential risks to inform us of the Legal Matrix are the Oracles. On another level, there are people who not only talk and teach, they perform acts that are courageous, criticized and sometimes misunderstood, all in the name of justice and freedom. Some of the Neo's are the public defenders, the men and women of congress who take unpopular positions and anyone else who constantly put themselves on the line for others.

Before we discuss some individual Neo's I want to mention a "Neo moment" I witnessed on television during a National basketball Association (NBA) half time show that featured a conversation and analysis of Dr. Martin Luther King Day, by Charles Barkley, Kenny Smith and Irvin "Magic" Johnson. The conversation was about the current NBA players and their understanding and appreciation of the work that was done by Martin Luther King Jr. First, I was impressed that these men would take the time on national television to have this conversation. Second, the compassion and the depth of the conversation impressed me. Third, the fact that many NBA fans, young and old, who were watching that evening received a bit of history and some inside information when they least expected to get such information, in the middle of a sporting event. That was the special thing about it. People were informed and lives possibly changed. Truly a Neo moment.

A standout example of a Neo is Martin Luther King Jr. He dedicated his life for the advancement of African Americans and all people. Ultimately he died for this same pursuit. I consider him a Neo not only because of his dedicated teachings, but because of his tireless work. Following in his footsteps is Barack Obama who sponsored the landmark bill in Illinois that requires videotaping police interrogations. Senator Obama said it is a win/win situation that helps "free the innocent but also convict the guilty." The expectation for his politic advancement is high, and based on his trailblazing efforts, rightfully so.

Below is a list of just some of the Neo's of our time. This list is not complete. There are many more, known and unknown who are just as important to our journey to success. If I listed all the Neo's who have affected my life, this text would be too voluminous.

Bishop Flanvis Josephus Johnson, Jr.

A dynamic speaker and educator, bold and intellectual. I have nothing but respect for the work of Bishop Flanvis Josephus Johnson, Jr. (Joey). He is the Founder and Senior Pastor of the House of the Lord in Akron, Ohio. Bishop is a noted conference speaker in the areas of the Bible, family, church growth (and management), business management, personal development and team building. Bishop Johnson's love for the Word of God is evident in his preaching and teaching which radiates power and drips with the anointing of God, making him a sought after revival speaker. He founded the Logos Bible Institute, Pastoral Mentoring Institute and Emmanuel Christian Academy to facilitate continual and in-depth Bible study for all ages. He released a book called "Family Mess," which was successful in helping people understand that God works through difficult circumstances. It is his hope that the message of the book will release people to pursue their hopes, dreams, expectations and destiny in the Holy Spirit.

Bishop Johnson is a Neo because he has dedicated his entire life to the freedom of people. His main goal is to bring people closer to the Lord and save souls, but his reach is even beyond that. Bishop Johnson was one of the first pastors to actual integrate *The Matrix* movie into his spiritual teachings and sermons. Many people who attend his church services leave motivated to be successful in their earthly pursuits as well as their Heavenly pursuit. His "real world" approach to teaching the word of God bridges the gap between a spiritual relationship with the Lord and the everyday life in America - the Legal Matrix. Bishop is my pastor and one of my Oracles and Neos.

Oprah Winfrey

Oprah Winfrey has already left an unforgettable, undeniable mark on the face of television. From her humble beginnings in rural Mississippi, Oprah Winfrey's legacy has established her as one of the most important figures in popular culture. Her contributions can be felt beyond the world of television and into areas such as publishing, music, film, philanthropy, education, health and fitness, and social awareness. As supervising producer and host of *The Oprah Winfrey Show,* Oprah Winfrey entertains, enlightens and empowers millions of viewers around the world.

Oprah Winfrey is involved in so much that the list would require most of this text, however, her credits include being the chairwoman of Harpo, Inc., Harpo Productions, Inc., Harpo Studios, Inc., Harpo Films, Inc., Harpo Print, LLC and Harpo Video, Inc.

I have been impressed by Oprah Winfrey for so many years that her inclusion in this book goes without question. I was most impressed by her recent trip to Africa. In December 2003, Ms. Winfrey began a gift-giving pilgrimage in Africa. On her trip, she gave away 50,000 Christmas gifts to orphans, and other desperately poor children. I watched the television with amazement and pride as I became part of her journey to the motherland providing gifts, encouragement, inspiration, and support. The reality is that Ms. Winfrey has accomplished much in her life. She has nothing else to prove to America or the world, but she continues to stretch beyond her comfort zone to bring hope to people. Ms. Winfrey is truly a Neo, a person here to help guide us to a more prosperous and successful life.

Oprah Winfrey says she was inspired by the nuns who brought food and gifts to her house on Christmas when she was just 12 years old. Moreover, not satisfied with just playing Santa once a year, Oprah Winfrey pledged to donate so to help build schools, empower women, and help fight AIDS in Africa. Ms. Winfrey's trip raised awareness about the AIDS epidemic. The statistics show that today, over 11 million children under the age of 15 living in sub-Saharan Africa have lost at least one parent to HIV/AIDS. UNICEF estimates that seven years from now the number will have grown to 25 million. At that point, anywhere from 15% to over 25% of the children in a dozen sub-Saharan African countries will be orphans -- the vast majority of which will have been orphaned by HIV/AIDS. "Ms. Winfrey has used her prominence to lend a voice to a silent crisis," said Charles J. Lyons, president of the U.S. Fund for UNICEF. "

Oprah Winfrey is a Neo because she continues to go against the grain. Whether it's by deciding to keep her television shows from becoming "smut T.V.," or by the way she make public stands and outcries against injustice, Oprah Winfrey has proven to be a source of inspiration for millions.

Sean "P Diddy" Combs

Sean Combs is the CEO of Bad Boy Enterprises which is a multi-business conglomerate including Bad Boy Records, Daddy's House Studios, Sean John Apparel line, and Justin's Restaurants. He even had a rendezvous into sports management and marketing. Sean Combs' business enterprise is worth an estimated $500 million. Not only does he produces platinum hits and has worked with almost every important name in music, he has been involved in television production.

In 2004, he ran the New York marathon to accomplish the task of raising over $2 million for the New York public schools. He embarked on a campaign called "Citizen Change" with the goal of motivating millions of young people across the nation to get involved in the voting process by first registering and then making their voice count.

Things have not always been perfect for the man, Sean Combs. Sean had a brush with the Legal Matrix when he faced 15 years in prison for weapons and bribery charges stemming from a 1999 nightclub shooting. Combs was able to handle the Legal Matrix. He assembled a team of great attorneys and made sure that he presented himself in the proper manner and worked within the system.

Time and time again in his career, Combs has shown the ability to bounce back when a problem or situation led him into the Legal Matrix. Earlier in his career, an event that he promoted ended up with many people injured and blaming Combs. As a Neo, he made it through. Then there was the East Coast/West Coast controversy and the death of his artist and friend, the Notorious B.I.G. Any or all of those situations would have destroyed a person with soft skin or lesser abilities, but Combs is a

196

Neo. He knows how to turn tragedy into triumph. He knows how to overcome the odds to ensure that his goals will be accomplished.

Whether you like his music, his appearances on MTV, his restaurants or image, there is no denying that Sean Combs is a man that has overcome the odds and has established himself as one of the most successful entrepreneurs in America today. Sean Combs is a Neo because he is a visionary. He shows us that hard work and relentless determination will overcome any disadvantage.

Jay Z

Jay-Z and Damon Dash together built an empire worth more than $300 million. Welcome to Roc-A-Fella Enterprises. The company is just about 8 years old and is comprised of Roc-A-Fella Records, Rocawear clothing and Roc-A-Fella Films, which has produced the movies *State Property* and *Paid in Full*. In addition to these accomplishments, Jay-Z has positioned himself as one of the greatest lyricists of all time and now is one of the heads of the music super conglomerate Def Jam Records.

What's notable about the work of Jay-Z is that he has moved from a poet who exposed the life of the ghetto to the masses, to a man who influences the way young urban men dress, think, and act. A famous line from one of his hits. "Like I told you to sell drugs, no, Hov did that so you *******." Life wasn't always so sweet for Jay-Z. He was born Shawn Corey Carter in 1969. He spent his childhood in the Marcy projects of Brooklyn. His father left him when he was 11, and he was raised by his mother, Gloria Carter. He admits that the height of the crack epidemic was a rough time: "Especially in that neighborhood. It was a plague in that neighborhood. It was just everywhere, everywhere you look. In the hallways. You could smell it in the hallways."

"Back then, I would say it was like two things," he adds. "It was either you're doin' it or you was movin' it."

It's an amazing achievement for a man who grew up in one of New York's toughest housing projects. As *60 Minutes II* told you last fall, he's living the 21st Century version of the American dream, straight out of the 'hood. Fifteen years ago, Jay-Z says he had no idea that he would be a wealthy superstar: "I had no aspirations, no plans, no goals, and no back-up goals." Jay-Z has already sold over 15 million albums, and his personal fortune is in upwards of $50 million.

But just as Jay-Z was beginning to be recognized as an entrepreneur, he fell victim to the Legal Matrix. In 1999, he stabbed record executive Lance Rivera at a nightclub. Police say he thought Rivera was bootlegging his music. He was sentenced to three years of probation. "I think it was a wake-up call, and the calling card for me that - to let me know, like, it could just all go down the drain; like, it could all be taken away from you," he says, promising it will never happen again.

That is what makes Jay-Z a Neo, he took his negative beginnings, a young man who did not know how he was going to survive, and through dedication and hard work, turned his life into the American dream.

Tupac Shakur

Tupac Shakur is an urban legion. His music still lives today and his message is still strong. Just the fact that we are able to hear new material from this slain man shows his immortal work ethic and dedication to his craft. Although Tupac Shakur lived a very dangerous life and often chose to live in the realm of danger or "thug life," he was an intellect, very well read, determined and sensitive individual. Most of our youth like to grasp the "thug life" movement and the "gansta" mentality, but Tupac Shakur was so much more than that.

In his record "Trapped," Tupac Shakur states: "can barely walk the city streets without a cop harassing me, searching me, and then asking my identity. Hands up, throw me up against the wall, didn't do a thing at all." The lyrics go on to discuss the destruction that occurred, the killing of the police officer "Who do you blame? It's a shame because the man was slain; he got caught in the chains of his own game. How can I feel guilty after all the things they did to me, sweated me, hunted me, and trapped me in my own community?"

He was raised as a socially conscious young man. Raised by a mother who was a part of the Black Panther movement, Tupac Shakur was thrust into the struggle of Black Americans. His music, teachings and dialog often spoke to and for the struggle of his people. His message and his teachings set him aside as a Neo. He took the outlet of music and used it to speak. His music was not just for entertainment. If you listened, it was to inform. In 1996, at the age of 25, he was shot to death in a car on the Las Vegas strip, however, his music lives on influencing and inspiring a generation of young people desperately trying to figure out the system that they live in, The Legal Matrix.

Tupac Shakur was deep, a socially conscious Neo who's life teachings and lessons, as we watched on television, can be instructive. Through his life we know that no matter how deep you are, no matter how talented you are, if you step out of line, the Legal Matrix will take you away.

Bill Maher

Bill Maher is one of the most politically astute humorists in America today. He never pulls a punch and is not afraid to stand up to any challenger, even in their face. His HBO show "Real Time with Bill Maher," has become a platform for honest discussion of political issues. He brings together the most interesting politicians, entertainers, and journalists to participate in some of the most controversial, topical and comical discussions.

This forging of different walks of life proves that we all have a voice, opinion and desire to make change. The Neo quality of the show is the fact that even with our most serious issues, Bill Maher is able to address them and keep the light hearted air that is necessary for serious change. Now that statement may seem odd, but it's true. Bill Maher teaches us that by working together and not taking ourselves too seriously we can truly move forward in this country.

Bill Clinton

During the administration of William Jefferson Clinton, the U.S. enjoyed more peace and economic well being than at any time in its history. He was the first Democratic president since Franklin D. Roosevelt to win a second term. He could point to the lowest unemployment rate in modern times, the lowest inflation in 30 years, the highest home ownership in the country's history, dropping crime rates in many places, and reduced welfare roles. He proposed the first balanced budget in decades and achieved a budget surplus. As part of a plan to celebrate the millennium in 2000, Clinton called for a great national initiative to end racial discrimination.

One of the Neo qualities of President Clinton is his ability to build bridges between the races. He was often refereed to as the "first black president," not only because of his ability to appeal to African Americans but also because of his ability to make African Americans from all walks of life feel a part of the governmental system. He gave Americans a sense of trust and comfort that is rare. He made us believe that the Legal Matrix was not only a system designed to control, but designed to help us be successful and secure.

Russell Simmons

Russell Simmons has emerged victorious in his battle against New York State's harsh drug laws, which had mandated 15 years to life for first-time low-level narcotics offenders, the toughest such minimum sentencing laws in the nation. He was able to assist in the lobbying of New York state legislators to the point where they voted to reduce penalties imposed by the so-called Rockefeller drug laws.

Reforming the laws has been an ongoing campaign, and in the past few years hip-hop artists and celebrities have joined the fray. Rap mogul Simmons got involved in 2003 when he gathered celebrity friends and rallied outside New York City Hall. The laws were enacted in 1973 when former New York Governor Nelson Rockefeller pushed statutes through the New York legislature to impose stiffer sentences on drug offenders. Governor George Pataki said he will sign the bipartisan legislative agreement, reached by Senate Majority Leader Joseph Bruno and State Assembly Speaker Sheldon Silver, which would reduce sentences for first-time. In addition, more than 400 inmates currently serving prison sentences based upon the prior mandates will be allowed to apply for early release.

Russell Simmons has done more than just work to change the drug laws; he has built an empire of successful businesses that rival many fortune 500 companies. On the civic side he has worked endlessly to rally millions of unregistered minorities to get registered and to get involved in the political system.

Russell Simmons has become a sought after voice and pundit on the "hip hop" generation. This man has lived a full life and again, he is a testament on what can be done and accomplished when you learn and work the Legal Matrix. From hip hop to the tip top, Russell Simmons is the godfather and a true Neo.

Judge Christine McMonagle

Judge McMonagle has a very big heart. That quality is uncommon for a judge in a felony court in one of the largest counties in the nation. Now ruling from the court of appeals, Judge McMonagle has the opportunity to shape the interpretation of our laws. Judge McMonagle has been on the bench several years and her work in the Legal Matrix has been as a good agent. She is known to be one of the fairest judges in the county. What does it take to be considered by your peers in the legal community as fair? Well she is a good listener, non prejudicial judge, and an intelligent legal pundit. She is tough on crime but also understanding when the time calls for it. Judge McMonagle is a judicial renegade and a true Neo, not just because she gave me guidance early in my career, but for many obvious reasons.

Judge Una Keenon

Judge Keenon has been on the bench in the City of East Cleveland for over 19 years. To appreciate her work, it must be understood that East Cleveland is one of the poorest cities in the country. In addition to being poverty stricken, the crime rate is ridiculous. Judge Keenon, regardless of the depressed area, is a shining staple in the community. Her dedication to the City of East Cleveland and the uplifting of her people is amazing. Judge Keenon overcame extreme racism and other problems to get to the position of judge. She now rules with an iron fist and a big heart. She often lectures her alleged criminals and hands out very unique sentences to ensure that they walk away from her courtroom with a fresh look and a new lease on life.

The Higher Spirit

Last but not least the greatest possible Oracle and Neo is your source of inspiration. For me it is my belief and reverence and devotion to Jesus Christ. It is through reading the word of God that I am able better understand my place, purpose and position in life. When there are questions, uncertainty or doubt, I go to prayer to find my way. Throughout time, the word of God has consistently guided people in times of despair. Through faith, it will continue to do so.

Freedom - The M.A.T.R.I.X System

The system is attacking. No need to worry excessively, it has always attacked. The difference is that throughout history we have been able to battle and gain wins. In every area of importance, Americans, through the legal system, have been able to fight for freedom. From the emancipation of slaves, the rights for Native Americans, the civil rights fights for African Americans, women's rights, the civil rights fights for gay and lesbians, the fights for civil liberties and education rights. This list goes on and on and the heroes of those fights are well known and documented. Now it is up to each one of us to continue to speak up for our rights. More importantly, understanding that the battle against the Legal Matrix is as much personal as it is public, we must develop ourselves in a manner that will guarantee our victory or at least our management of the system.

There is a saying that "he who can not change the very fabric of his thought will never be able to change reality, and, will never, therefore, make any progress." Anwar Sadat. In order to win the war against the Legal Matrix we must first develop our mind to win. Let's look at a few ways to win the war against the Legal Matrix. The theory is called M.A.T.R.I.X. Mastering your Actions, techniques, responsibility and intellect to excel.

MASTERY OF ACTIONS:

Develop a Positive Attitude

Your focus is your reality. That is a simple statement full of power and strength. If you want to be an all American athlete – focus on it. If you want to be a lawyer – focus on it. If you want to be a teacher – focus on it. But by all means never focus on the negative. To often people fail to recognize the impact and power of a positive mental attitude. In fact, these same people often fail to recognize the power of attitude in general. Attitude or the way that you look at a situation or life, guides your emotions which then guide your actions. It is a three step process and outlined in the Legal Matrix workbook.

The attitude is the way in which we see our environment and our circumstances. It was said by Anwar Sadot that if a man can not change the very fabric of his thought than he can not change his situation. I am paraphrasing, but the point should be clear. If we begin or go into a situation from a negative perspective then the same result will follow. Negative attitudes breed negative emotions which then produce negative actions by people. When a situation or circumstance is looked at from a negative perspective, there is a danger of bad outcomes.

The same is true for positive attitudes. We have the opportunity to react to any and every situation the way that we chose. There is a lot of power in that little space of time between the action and our response or reaction to it.

By utilizing the power of a positive attitude and the space that allows you to react properly to a situation, you will gain freedom from the Legal Matrix and the web of disaster.

Be Mindful of Your Thoughts and Create Balance

The way that we perceive ourselves and the Legal Matrix will determine how we travel through life's journey. Our thoughts will guide us. If you think that the system is stacked against you, that you are a victim who cannot control his/her life, then that is what life will hand you. Being positive that you can be successful regardless of the obstacles will result in you winning the game.

Remember, (I said earlier that) the Legal Matrix can not control the most precious, and valuable resource that we have – our mind. The Legal Matrix can not stop you from being creative, analyzing situations, and strategizing a way out of the web. By keeping your head high and your thoughts positive, the Legal Matrix can be handled.

MASTERY OF TECHNIQUES:

Have Proper Support

The importance of support is based on the fact that in order to survive challenges, we all need a strategy that will lead us to victory. It is a good ideal to have a group of people, places, or things that can assist you in your difficult times. If there is a group of people whom you rely on, make sure everyone is on the same page with you. When the Legal Matrix strikes, you need individuals who will work with you and not against you. Depending on your situation, you may need financial support, you may need emotional support. Whatever it is that you need, your support group and those you trust should be able to help you through.

Another important component to your support and strategy is to hire a competent attorney to represent you, and you must pay your attorney. It's important to find an attorney that you can trust. Attorney-client relationships have become too informal. Clients look at attorneys as quick fixes while attorneys look at clients as a paycheck.

I have developed a practice where I am not just providing legal advice to my clients; I also participate in development and planning. Accordingly, I am both an attorney at law and a life strategist. I take the opportunity to really help people and I form relationships with my client whereby I am still a paid performer, but at the same time I have an interest in my clients overall well being.

The Legal Matrix

When you hire your attorney, make sure that he is someone that you can trust. Many clients don't tell their attorneys all or even enough information to properly provide a defense or legal representation. Information is the key to a successful relationship with your attorney. I cannot tell you how many times I was stuck in a position where I did not have enough information, or I had the wrong information. I had clients in domestic violence cases; tell me that there was no physical exchange, and that the other party would not testify against them. Then, in the middle of a hearing, I find that the other person is going to testify about the physical exchange and that there are pictures, witnesses, and other evidence that leans toward my client's guilt. You must be honest with yourself and your team in order to deal with the Legal Matrix.

Once you select an attorney, look to determine whether or not he or she is able to disconnect the emotion. Good Lawyers are able to disconnect the emotion. When the case is up and it is time to go to trial, it does not matter that the client is a difficult person, it does not matter that the client did not pay, it does not matter what is happening on other cases or at home. It is time to fight. When it is time to fight, make sure your attorney is a true advocate. By true advocate, I mean that he or she is ready and willing to put forth a fight when the time is right. When your attorney steps in the courtroom on your behalf he should transform into a bulldog whose main goal is to get the best outcome for his client. Otherwise, your attorney is useless and your team is weak.

There was a situation where I was asked by one of my favorite judges – Dean Buchanan in the City of Cleveland Heights, to represent a man charged with menacing. He was an older white male and the victim was an African American female. The charges were based on words, racial epithets that the male said to the woman. They were both entering a business parking lot, and apparently going for the same parking space. The African American woman made it to the parking space first. Allegedly, the white male rode up behind her and started making racial remarks and telling her that it was his parking space, because he was there first, and that she had to move. While I read the police report, the witness statements, and listened to the prosecutor summarize the events, I was shocked at the words that I heard and the fact that I was about to represent a man who, for all intents and purposes, was a racist. This is where being a good attorney comes in. I had to represent him. Just imagine if I did not, I would have set African Americans back 100 years! Think if every white attorney who felt uncomfortable with African Americans did not represent them, justice would have not prevailed for many years, or at least until there was one African American attorney for every person. We would have been left without proper representation. In this case, I decided to represent the man. I looked at this case as I do all my other cases. I put the emotionalism aside. This man deserved a fair hearing and an assurance that his rights are not violated by the Legal Matrix. So I did my best and gave him my best legal advice.

MASTERY OF RESPONSIBILITY:

For everything that happens to us, there is a response that we have. If we maser or response ability, we will have better success in the Legal Matrix. Our attitude shapes our response. If we are predisposed to look at the situation from a positive perspective, then the time between the action and our response will be used to reflect in a positive manner thus giving the likelihood of a positive outcome. For example, your boss comes in to work and accuses you of stealing some of the company products. Before you respond to the accusations, there is a space of time that you have to ponder your response. Now if you are a positive thinker you will say something to the effect of "of course he is mistaken, but maybe he has bad information." then you will give him a calm response. On the other hand, if your attitude leads you to say "I'm sick of being blamed for stuff, I hate this job." then your response will enviably be negative.

Understanding that we have the opportunity to use the space between an action and our response and further, knowing that there is power in that space. Let me give you some important facts. The space is either large or small. If you are facing a gun pointed to your head, the space is obviously small. If you received a voicemail after work, and don't have to respond until the morning, then the space is large. The length of the space is also dictated by your attitude. If you have a positive attitude, you will be able to control the desire to immediately respond to an attack.

However, if you lack the positive attitude, there is a greater likelihood that you will respond to an attack with an immediate attack of your own. It's just something about being attacked that makes people respond.

MASTERY OF INTELLECT:

Seek Knowledge

Knowledge unfits a child to be a slave - Frederick Douglas.

In order to coincide with the Legal Matrix you must first acknowledge that it exists. By ignoring its existence or being ignorant to it, we are unable to live productively with it. Living productively with the Legal Matrix is the key to freedom. When you decided to take the red pill and travel with me into the inner workings of the system that affects every part of our lives – the Legal Matrix, you opened up you mind to the possibilities of true freedom. True freedom comes with knowledge. To gain knowledge was an understanding that African Americans in the 40's, 50's and 60's held on to and taught to each generation. My mother told me numerous times to "learn all you can, no one can ever take your knowledge from you."

It is not necessary to know all the rules of the Legal Matrix, that's what attorneys are for (at least we try), but you need to be aware of its existence, and the fact that it will cause your demise if you are not mindful of it. To know the system does not require an advanced education. It only requires that you take the time to recognize the environment in which you live. Know the rules of your game, know the laws that affect you and your life. If you are in a special vocation, sport, or industry, know the rules that will ensure your success in that area so that you are not blindsided by mishaps. Most importantly, know the consequences of adverse actions. If you are going to take risks, then you should know the consequences of that choice.

Learning the error of our ways – The Michael Jackson Effect

We must attack and defeat our own ignorance by making ourselves and everyone around us aware of the Legal Matrix. One of the biggest problems that I see on a daily basis is our inability to learn from our mistakes. Once we have experienced the wrath or potential wrath of the system, we must enact our ability to learn from this exposure and to stay out of trouble. A prime example is the felonious assault case that I mentioned earlier. I won the case where the wife ran her car into her husband's mistress, but the shocking part is that after all of that "drama" these parties did not separate from each other - none of them did. A few months after the case was over, I ran into the wife and husband independently. I was told by the wife that she and the husband are still together though not living together, that they have been having sex in the home of the girlfriend and that she and the girlfriend still get into confrontations about the husband. When I ran into the husband, I was told that he is still with both women, though not living with either full time. In other words, he spends time with each woman and lives between both houses. Additionally, he told me that he continues to go through "drama" with each woman, and he still receives financial support from each one. Just as in the original case, this situation is a time bomb waiting to happen. Either someone will end up in jail, hurt or dead. I took the time to express that sentiment to each party but I believe my information fell on deaf ears. They did not learn the error of their ways.

The Michael Jackson Effect

Where did Michael Jackson go wrong? I will not use this text to further damage or criticize an entertainer that I admired as a child; however, there is a less on to be learned in from his current legal situation. Never expose yourself to danger, and if you do, don't do it again. Michael was accused of questionable relations with young boys before his 2005 criminal trial. He was investigated, humiliated, sued, and forced to pay large sums of money. None of those events made him think "I shouldn't get myself into this again." He did not learn from his mistake and he continued to expose himself by being alone with young boys.

Whether your situation is one of relationship destruction or another type, we need to be able to learn from our mistakes and then walk away. Bad relationships are worse than some bad habits. So we must learn the error of our ways and avoid negative temptation. Temptation, though it can be managed, is too strong to ignore. Temptation to stay in a bad relationship; temptation to continue dangerous relationships; temptation to continue selling drugs for the fast money; temptation to sexual desires; temptation of the *thrill;* temptation to use drugs; temptation to disobey the law and not play the game the way it must be played.

The only way to master the Legal Matrix is to use our inner strength to beat it. Use the one thing that it is unable to control our minds. The system can create the playing field, the rules can change, the circumstances can switch, but knowledge and ability to use our mind and learn from our mistakes remains our strongest tool to master the Legal Matrix.

Engage the Unknown - We Must Attempt to Live Productively with the Legal Matrix

Independence from the Legal Matrix is really a misnomer. There is no true independence - meaning that we are all and will all be subject to the Legal Matrix itself. Independence comes from being knowledgeable about the system. Knowledge is power and through that power we can practice and strive for independence. The key is to make sure that the Legal Matrix does not capture you. When you are in the middle of the turmoil it can drain your energy, drive, and creativity.

The Legal Matrix is full of unknowns. In order to be success in the Legal Matrix we must get to know it. To get to know the Legal Matrix, we must engage the unknown. Welcome The challenge of learning about the system. Be encouraged by the fact that once we engage the unknown, knowledge, understanding and success will come.

The information and theories presented in this book will not save you from the Legal Matrix, but instead it will give you the knowledge necessary to form individual plans to co-exist with it. Now that we know it is here, now that we know our liberties can and will be taken away if we do not protect them, go out and live life to the fullest, inform others about the Legal Matrix, and become a Neo in your own personal life.

EXCELL:

Once we master the matrix we will excel in everything that we do. Here are a few additional was to ensure that we excel in the Legal Matrix.

Build Bridges

Many religious pundits, politicians, community activists, and people from every walk of life are trying to solve the problems in life and the community by working at it alone. These people fail to understand that we (human beings) are relational beings. We were created based on a relationship and exist to experience relationships. There is no way that we can be successful in the Legal Matrix without reaching out to others and using their resources to win freedom. There was a time when I considered running for Mayor of the city where I was born and raised. The desire to be Mayor came from my deep earning to help make change and improve the lives of my people. That is how we must approach success in the Legal Matrix. Every time one of us fall victim to the web of the Matrix, we are exposing every other person to web. When we do not work to ensure the safety of all, the civil rights of all, the well being of all we are working for the destruction of our peace and happiness.

One of the major theories behind building bridges is the acknowledgement that we can not survive alone. And even if we do, we will not find true success or happiness. Bill Gates is not a Billionaire because he created a software product and then decided not to share it with anyone else. No, he gave it to the world and in fact, through his foundation, he continues to give to people and communities throughout this nation and beyond. That is the success that comes from building bridges.

The way to build bridges is to begin to help in the little things. Give a little more attention to detail at work. Stay longer with your family, give more tithes to church, and spend a little more time in your studies. By helping and giving to others, we will build the bridges necessary to be successful in the Legal Matrix. My profession is built on building bridges; you can not be an attorney with out the desire to build the bridge

Work the System

One of my favorite pastors, R.A.Veronon from the Word Church in Cleveland Ohio told his congregation to "work that thang." His use of the slang word "thang" drove home the point that your desire, goals, and aspirations are uniquely yours. You have to own it and then work it.

The premise behind "working your thang," and working the system is that you must aggressively get involved in making the change necessary to be successful. You must aggressively get involved in the process of gaining the knowledge necessary to be successful. You must go to the limits to achieve. Make all necessary calls, meet the right people, and don't stop pushing.

Take Responsibility

Although we have been told from early childhood that we should be willing to take responsibility for our actions, somewhere in our development to adulthood, many of us lost sight of the responsibility factor. In courtrooms, boardrooms and every other conceivable place in this country there are people who are not taking responsibility for their place in life.

The failure to take responsibility is a road block to success against the Legal Matrix. Too many people blame the system for their problems. In my practice as a lawyer, I constantly hear excuses like "the police officer did not arrest the other person," "She made me do it," "the officer should not have pulled over my car." The examples are endless. The bottom line is that too many people have excuses for their mistakes. The alternative is to take responsibility. Acknowledge the reasons that are behind a particular situation and then you will be able to deal with the facts and come to a true resolution. Until you own your problem, you will not be able to solve the problem. Just like an addict must admit to the addiction or he will never be able to beat it.

This book will not save anyone, we must all save ourselves. This book is presented truthfully and without fear so that you can be prepared to deal with the challenges of the Legal Matrix and be successful. It is easy to live without this awareness, but it becomes painful when the system is thrown on you.

The Fight Continues in the Next Episode:

The Legal Matrix
"Reloaded"
What You Don't Know Will Hurt You !

---

[i] Robert Hodierne, The Military Times, December 6, 2004

[ii] Bishop Joey Johnson, House of the Lord Church, Akron, Ohio
[iii] The legal team of James Willis, Fernando Mack, Myron Watson, William Dawson
[iv] *U.S. v. Dionisio*, 410 U.S. 1 (1973)
[v] Costello v. U.S., 350 U.S. 359 (1956)
[vi] U.S. v. Williams, 504 U.S. 36 (1992
[vii] Handbook for Federal Grand Juries, U.S. District Court of New York
[viii] *United States v. Calandra* 414 U.S. 338 (1974)
[ix] *United States v. Leibowitz*, 420 F.2d 39 (2d Cir. 1969)
[x] *United States v. Trass*, 644 F.2d 791 (9th Cir. 1981)
[xi] *United States v. Williams*, 112 S.Ct. 1735 (1992),
[xii] U.S. Sentencing Commission

[xiii] AP January 1, 2004

[xiv] *Maryland v. Pringle,* 370 Md. 525 (2003)
[xv] The 9th International Anticorruption Conference, presentation by Thomas Kubic Deputy Assistant Director FBI
[xvi] New York Times, William K. Rashbaum, March 11, 2005.
[xvii] New York Times, December 19, 1995 *Police Corruption and Brutality: What's the Link, Gerald Smith.*
[xviii] *State of Ohio v. Berry*, 1999 (10th App. Distr., Frankl. Co. 1999)

[xix] Sec. 530. Payment of travel and transportation expenses of newly appointed special agents

> The Attorney General or the Attorney General's designee is authorized to pay the travel expenses of newly appointed special agents and the transportation expenses of their families and household goods and personal effects from place of residence at time of selection to the first duty station, to the extent such payments are authorized by section 5723 of title 5 for new appointees who may receive payments under that section. (Added Pub. L. 98-86, Sec. 1, Aug. 26, 1983, 97 Stat. 492.)

[xx] The Center for Public Integrity, June 26, 2003

xxi The Center for Public Integrity, June 26, 2003
xxii CBS.com June 26, 2003

xxiii In Spite of Innocence: Erroneous Convictions in Capital Cases," Michael L Radelet, HugoAdam Bedau, and Constance E. Putnam, Northeastern University Press, Boston, 1996 pb ed. with new forward, 331 (© 1992).

xxiv Criminal Prosecution Reform Website by Carl E. Person
xxv *Gates v. Illinois,* 462 U.S. 213 (1983).
xxvi *U.S. v. Leon,* 468 U.S. 897 (1984).
xxvii January 4, CBS's "60 Minutes"
xxviii US Sentencing Commission. (1995, February). *Special Report to Congress: Cocaine and Federal Sentencing Policy,* Table, 18. Washington, DC: U.S. Sentencing Commission, pg. 170
xxix January 4, CBS's "60 Minutes"
xxx January 4, CBS's "60 Minutes"
xxxi Association of Americans for Constitutional Laws and Justice
xxxii Brenda Grantland, "Your House Is Under Arrest," Institute for the Preservation of Wealth, Burnsville, Minn., 1993
xxxiii "Forfeiture Law Hits Innocent Citizens," Jack Anderson and Michael Binstein
xxxiv *Oliver v. United States,* 466 U.S. 170 (1984).
xxxv *United States v. Dunn,* 107 S.Ct. 1134 (1987).
xxxvi *California v. Ciraolo,* 476 U.S. 207 (1986); Florida v. Riley, 488 U.S. 445 (1989).
xxxvii *United States v. Miller,* 425 U.S. 435 (1976).
xxxviii *Smith v. Maryland,* 442 U.S. 735 (1979).
xxxix *United States v. White,* 401 U.S. 745 (1971).
xl *California v. Greenwood,* 486 U.S. 25 (1988).

xli *Olmsted v. United States.*

xlii Washington Associated Press, reported on USA Today.com 8/1/05
xliii Pittsburgh Post-Gazette.

xliv *Maryland v. Pringle,* 370 Md. 525 (2003)
xlv Chris Seay *The Gospel Reloaded.*

xlvi *Undercover: Police Surveillance in America (20th Century Fund) by Gary T. Marx*
xlvii *The Soft Cage - Surveillance in America from Slavery to the War on Terror.*